Collective Biographies

American Heroes of Exploration and Flight

Anne Schraff

Enslow Publishers, Inc.

40 Industrial Road   PO Box 38
Box 398   Aldershot
Berkeley Heights, NJ 07922   Hants GU12 6BP
USA   UK

http://www.enslow.com

Library of Congress Cataloging-in-Publication Data

Schraff, Anne E.
    American heroes of exploration and flight / Anne Schraff.
        p. cm. — (Collective biographies)
    Includes bibliographical references and index.
    Summary: A collection of biographies of ten American adventurers
  including Robert Peary, Amelia Earhart, Neil Armstrong, and Christa McAuliffe.
    ISBN 0-89490-619-4
    1. Air pilots—United States—Biography—Juvenile literature.
  2. Explorers—United States—Biography—Juvenile literature.
  [1. Air pilots. 2. Astronauts. 3. Explorers.] I. Title. II. Series.
  TL539.S34 1995
  629.13'092'273—dc20
  [B]   95-13466
                                      CIP
                                      AC

Printed in the U.S.A.

10 9 8 7 6 5 4 3

Illustration Credits:
Library of Congress, pp. 6, 16, 23, 26, 36, 46; National Aeronautics and Space
Administration (NASA), pp. 66, 73, 76, 81, 86, 93, 96, 103; San Diego
Aerospace Museum, pp. 13, 43, 53, 56, 63; United States Navy, p. 33.

Cover Illustration:
National Aeronautics and Space Administration (NASA)

Contents

Preface

Throughout human history, the spirit of adventure has stimulated men and women to explore, investigate, and—if need be—take risks with their very lives. Some of this spirit is in most human hearts. But in a rare few, this spirit has been a motivator to great and historic deeds. These few people had what President Ronald Reagan found in the crew of the *Challenger* space shuttle "that special grace, that special spirit that says 'give me a challenge and I'll meet it with joy.'"[1]

This sense of joy in adventure appears like a shining thread throughout lives as diverse as the people featured in this book. The Wright brothers remained at heart small boys playing with toy helicopters until their childhood fantasies became reality. Charles Lindbergh, Amelia Earhart, and Jackie Cochran also found joy in aviation. Earhart titled her book *For the Fun of It*, cutting to the core of an aviator's heart.

Polar explorers Matthew Henson, Robert Peary, and Richard Byrd all experienced joy in their adventures. Byrd admitted that the joy he drew from exploring his icy world dominated his life.

Space pioneers Neil Armstrong, Sally Ride, Guion Bluford, and Christa McAuliffe delighted in space adventures. Sally Ride expressed the emotion best when asked what she will remember most about her first flight. "The thing that I'll remember most about the flight is that it was fun."[2]

The sheer joy of placing a footprint on clean, shining, unmarked snow in the polar regions; or of seeing from space the beautiful blue ball that is Earth; or of being alone in a tiny wind-battered plane crossing an ocean or a continent overcame the fears these people surely felt.

These rare souls, whose adventures are told here, have—like brilliant comets—streaked through our lives; brightening them with their glory, and in no small way, taking the rest of us with them on their incredible journeys. For most of us, these adventures will inspire us with awe and admiration. For a few of us, they will point the way to similar adventures of our own, challenging some yet distant frontier.

Orville and Wilbur Wright

Orville and Wilbur Wright

The Flying Brothers

In the autumn of 1878 eleven-year-old Wilbur Wright and his seven-year-old brother, Orville, crowded excitedly around their father, who concealed a toy in his hands. Suddenly their father cast the toy into the air. It flew across the room until it struck the ceiling, briefly fluttering before sinking to the floor. The toy was called a helicopter, but the Wrights called it "the bat." This small flying object instantly became the Wrights' favorite toy.[1]

Wilbur Wright was born on April 16, 1867, on a small farm at Millsville, Indiana. He was the third son in the family. His father, Milton Wright, a minister, later took the family to Dayton, Ohio. There,

Orville Wright was born on August 19, 1871. Sister Katharine was born in 1874.

As a boy, Orville was full of mischief. In fact, at the end of his sixth-grade year, he was dismissed for misbehaving. Only after much pleading was Orville allowed back to enter seventh grade. He then earned the highest arithmetic score of any student in Dayton. Curious and inventive, Orville was like his father, who once made a crude typewriter, and his mother Susan, who designed and made her own clothing.

Brother Wilbur read adventure stories and was a fine athlete. He played baseball and hockey, and was the best gymnast in Dayton. He was also sensitive. When Wilbur saw Orville making woodcuts (engravings on wood) using an old pocket knife, Wilbur bought his younger brother a set of engraving tools the next Christmas.

When Wilbur was twelve and Orville was eight, they set out to earn pocket money by selling used articles to a local junkyard. Having no means to haul the old metal and wooden items that they had collected from their neighbors to the junkyard, they built a wagon out of two old tricycles and a wagon bed. Their mother advised them to polish the working parts with axle grease, giving them an early lesson in reducing friction.

In their teens, the Wrights invented a machine to help them fold their church newspaper every week. At age twelve, Orville teamed with another friend to publish a school newspaper. It was called

The Midget because it was only three inches wide by four and a half inches long. *The Midget* was not a success, so Orville bought a bigger press to turn out handbills and another newspaper, the *West Side News.*

Neither Wilbur nor Orville ever officially graduated from high school, but both boys were in a hurry to make their mark in the world. Orville was a pale young man with fine regular features. He was impulsive and enthusiastic, but shy before strangers. Wilbur was darker and more striking looking, with sharp features. He was also more outgoing than his brother as well as being a voracious reader with a fabulous memory.[2]

The Wrights opened a bicycle shop where they sold and repaired bikes. Before long they were building their own bicycles. In 1885, when Wilbur was eighteen, he was seriously injured playing hockey. While recovering, he developed heart trouble. For the next eight years Wilbur was an invalid. He spent his time reading—often about aviation. He read about the bold flight experiments of Otto Lilienthal in Germany and Octave Chanute in America.

When Wilbur regained his health in 1893, the Wrights remembered their childhood toy—"the bat." They began to experiment with kits and gliders, and they watched birds. Orville said, "We could not understand that there was anything about a bird that would enable it to fly that could not be built on a larger scale and used by man."[3]

In 1896 Otto Lilienthal was fifty feet above the ground when a gust of wind struck his glider, causing the glider to crash. Lilienthal received fatal spine injuries. The dying man said, "Sacrifices must be made!"[4] Lilienthal's death made the Wrights even more determined to crack the secret of flight. They studied Chanute's *Progress in Flying Machines* and other books on aerodynamics. They were appalled at how many had already died trying to achieve flight.

The Wrights strove for controlled flight, not just wind-driven gliding. Because of their obsession with their dream, they rejected social lives and marriage. Wilbur Wright explained that he did not have time for both a wife and an airplane.[5]

In the spring of 1899 Octave Chanute, now a friend of the Wrights, suggested that they experiment with their gliders in the Carolinas. The Wrights consulted the United States Weather Bureau (now the National Weather Service), and narrowed the choice down to Kitty Hawk, North Carolina. Wilbur strode miles of sand dunes there, searching for the ideal spot. Then, in 1901, both Wrights went to Kitty Hawk and pitched a tent. During the day they took turns lying prone on the lower wing of a double-winged glider, flying for about two minutes. By July of the same year they had built a larger glider. While gliding one day, Wilbur Wright hit the sand almost exactly like Lilienthal had. Fortunately, Wilbur was unhurt.

Discouraged by the near-fatal accident, the Wrights returned to their bicycle business, but they continued to experiment with flight concepts. In the winter of 1901–1902 they built a wind tunnel to test two hundred different types of wing surfaces.

In August 1902 the Wrights had a new glider at Kitty Hawk, which they flew unmanned for three hours. They made twenty-five flights, but the glider kept diving into the sand—no matter how they warped the wings. Orville then put a movable rudder in the tail, and the Wrights made one thousand more glides. They had solved the mystery of balance and control. Now they needed just one more thing—an engine. The Wrights had an engine built to their specifications and returned to Kitty Hawk with glider, engine, and propellers. Assembling all the parts took three weeks. Then, in December 1903, they were ready for the crucial trial flight.

The Wrights laid a long wooden rail on the windy side of Kill Devil Hill so that the plane would have a smooth surface to slide on before taking off. The brothers tossed a coin on who would first fly the plane. Wilbur Wright won. He lay on the wing, and the plane rose a few feet. But then it plunged into the sand, snapping a skid (a device used to check the wheels' turning). Three days of repair were necessary before another flight could be tried.

On December 17, 1903, the brothers returned to Kill Devil Hill. Puddles of water from a recent rain were ice-covered, and a bitterly cold wind blew. The Wrights invited spectators, but only five braved the chill. Wilbur had already had his turn, so now

Orville lay down on the lower wing and pushed the small lever. As the plane began to move down the track, Wilbur ran alongside, holding one wing to balance the machine. Suddenly the plane rose into the air, soaring high over Wilbur's head. This historic first flight, in the brothers' words:

> . . . lasted only twelve seconds, a flight very modest compared with that of birds, but it was nevertheless the first in the history of the world in which a machine carrying a man had raised itself by its own power into the air in free flight, had sailed forward on a level course without reduction of speed, and had finally landed without being wrecked.[6]

After the first flight, the Wrights tried four more. Then a sudden gust of wind abruptly struck the engine-propelled glider, seriously damaging it. "The machine rolled over and over," lamented Wilbur. "The ribs in the surfaces of the machine were broken, the motor injured."[7]

Fearing that their idea would be stolen before a United States Patent was secured (they had applied for one), the Wrights did not seek a lot of publicity. However, they sent this telegram to their father: "Success four flights, Thursday morning all against twenty-one-mile wind. Started from level with engine power alone. Inform press."[8]

Their father said, "Neither could have mastered the problem alone. As inseparable as twins, they are indispensable to each other."[9]

The Wright brothers tested their first flyer at Kitty Hawk, North Carolina, on December 17, 1903.

Wilbur agreed. "Orville and myself lived together, worked together, and, in fact, thought together."[10]

In January 1904 the Wrights invited fifty people to an airfield near Dayton, Ohio. The guests were to watch them fly their newer and bigger plane, but the flight was a failure. Now the Wrights were ridiculed by many who suggested that the flight at Kitty Hawk had been a hoax. The brothers doggedly continued perfecting their invention. Word spread that those "crazy Wright boys" were actually flying their machines. Dayton citizens often looked toward the sky to see them flying.

In August 1907 the Wrights had their patent and hoped to sell their invention to the United States Army. In May 1908 the Wrights took up their first passenger, Charles W. Furnas, in their new two-passenger plane. Orville Wright remained in the United States to try to meet government specifications for a plane, while Wilbur went to France to begin flying from a race track near Le Mans. Even now the brothers shunned publicity, but large crowds gathered to watch Wilbur Wright fly.[11]

On September 17, 1908, Orville Wright took a young West Point graduate, Thomas Selfridge, aboard as a passenger at Fort Myer, Virginia. The plane crashed, severely injuring Wright and killing Selfridge. Selfridge became the first person to die in heavier-than-air flight. As Orville recovered from his injuries, Wilbur wrote of ten thousand cheering people at Camp D'Auvours near Le Mans, applauding his record-breaking flights.

In 1909 the Wright brothers and their sister Katharine toured Paris, Rome, and London to parades and fireworks. In that year the Wrights met the Army's specifications and formed the Wright Company to make airplanes at a Dayton factory. Wilbur became company president, while Orville went to Montgomery, Alabama, to start a flying school to train pilots.

In May 1910 the Wrights took their eighty-two-year-old father for his first flight. Between 1909 and 1910 financial success finally came for the Wrights, but they resented all the time spent on business details. They faced harrowing legal fights to protect their patent. After one very bitter patent suit, Wilbur came home exhausted. Having eaten some contaminated shellfish, he soon became fatally ill. Orville blamed Wilbur's death on his weakened physical condition. In 1912 Wilbur, at the age of forty-five, was laid to rest. Twenty-five thousand mourners hailed Wilbur Wright as the co-inventor of the airplane and as a father of flight.

Orville never again seriously experimented, devised, or invented anything—even though he was only forty-one. He lived quietly until his death from a heart attack on January 30, 1948. The famous flying machine used at Kill Devil Hill was enshrined at the Smithsonian Institution in Washington, D.C. The Wright brothers of Ohio had ushered in the era of aviation.

Matthew Henson

Matthew Henson and Robert Peary

Companions at the Pole

Above the two men a lifeless gray sky was nearly black at the horizon. All around them the ice was a ghostly chalky white. The two explorers were now three nautical miles from the North Pole—the goal both had been seeking for the last twenty years. Matthew Henson saw Lieutenant Robert Peary's jaw square. "I was sure he was satisfied," Henson said. "Feeling that the time had come I ungloved my hand and went forward to congratulate him."[1]

Peary was so blinded by the snow that he did not see his companion's hand, admitting later, "I was actually too exhausted to realize at the moment that my life's purpose had been achieved."[2]

Matthew Alexander Henson, an African American, was born August 8, 1866, in Charles County, Maryland. He was the son of freeborn sharecroppers. At age four, Matthew was taken to Washington, D.C., by his parents. Within a few years both parents died, leaving him and several siblings to be raised by an uncle.

Matthew left school at age thirteen to seek his fortune at the Baltimore shipyards. He hoped to sign aboard a ship. He soon met an elderly sea captain who hired him as a cabin boy. Matthew was bright, hardworking, and strong. He proved to be a fine seaman on voyages to China, Japan, North Africa, and the Black Sea. During the long trips he studied geography, mathematics, history, classics, and the Bible under the captain. Matthew also had a gift for foreign languages.

In 1884, when Henson was eighteen, the sea captain died, forcing the young man reluctantly to return to land. For the next two years Henson worked at odd jobs. In 1886 he returned to Washington, D.C., and found a clerking job at Stinemetz & Sons Furriers. He was good at his tasks of keeping inventory and storing furs, and he earned the respect of his employers. But Henson's heart was elsewhere, yearning for adventure. He did not know it yet, but soon the greatest adventure of his life would begin with a man coming through the furrier's doors.

Robert Edwin Peary, an only child, was born May 6, 1856, in Cresson, Pennsylvania. When Robert's father died in 1858, his mother took him to be near her parents in Maine. As a boy, Robert was adventurous, hiking through the woods and pretending that he was an explorer. He collected rocks and plants and carefully noted them in his diary.

As Robert grew older he wrote poetry. Bright and athletic, he was excellent in school. Robert's particular interest in mathematics grew when he reached his teens, so he decided to study engineering.

When Peary was eighteen he earned a scholarship to study civil engineering at Bowdoin College in Brunswick, Maine. He was awarded a Phi Beta Kappa key for outstanding academic achievement. After graduation in 1877, he moved to Washington, D.C., to work as a draftsman for the United States Coast and Geodetic Survey Office.

At the age of twenty-four, Peary said, "I don't want to live and die without accomplishing anything or without being known beyond a narrow circle of friends."[3] He became an engineer for the United States Navy in 1881 and was sent to the jungles of Nicaragua to help clear the way for a proposed canal. On his way to Nicaragua, Peary passed the island of San Salvador—the first shoreline visible to Columbus in the New World. Peary wrote: "The fame of Columbus in the New World will be equaled only by the man who stands at the top of the world—the discoverer of the North Pole."[4]

Peary had a childhood fascination with arctic travel. He read many books on polar explorers. While browsing in a bookstore in 1885, he found a pamphlet describing Swedish explorations in Greenland. In 1886 the thirty-year-old Peary took a leave of absence from the Navy to reconnoiter the Greenland ice cap east of Disco Bay. That summer he sailed an area of Greenland two hundred miles north of the Arctic Circle to determine if it was possible to reach the North Pole by an overland route. Braving danger and surviving several narrow escapes, Peary made the first recorded journey to the interior ice cap of lower arctic Greenland on July 15, 1886.

Peary returned to Washington, D.C., with excellent maps of Greenland, which were praised by scientists. This gave Peary his first taste of popular acclaim. He lectured around the country and was elected to the American Society for the Advancement of Science. After two years Peary was again assigned to Nicaragua. In preparation for his departure, he took a collection of valuable furs that he had acquired in Greenland to store at the furriers Stinemetz & Sons.

Peary had been to the furriers before and he had struck up a friendship with the clerk—Matthew Henson—who shared his hunger for adventure. Often the two men would trade travel tales. Now Peary asked the twenty-two-year-old Henson to become his personal assistant on the journey to Nicaragua. Peary was impressed with Henson's skills as a navigator, mechanic, and carpenter. Henson was delighted to abandon his desk, and soon the two were off to Nicaragua.

With a mutual admiration for one another, Peary said of Henson that he had "intelligence, faithfulness, and better than average pluck and endurance."[5]

Henson said of Peary, "I recognized in him the qualities that made me willing to engage myself in his service."[6]

After Nicaragua, Henson and Peary went their separate ways—but not for long. They had forged strong bonds and soon adventure united them again. Peary was now seriously pursuing his North Pole dream and he wanted Henson with him.

By 1889 Peary was married to Josephine Diebitsch, and in 1891, Henson wed Eva Helen Flint. But when the opportunity to explore northwest Greenland came, neither hesitated to leave home. In June 1891 Henson and Peary boarded the *Barkentine Kite*. As well-wishers cheered, the two sailed toward Greenland.

Henson had far more experience at sea than anyone else in Peary's party. He loved sailing in the two hundred and eighty ton *Barkentine Kite*, with its huge white sails and seven-knot steam engine.

After coaxing the *Barkentine Kite* through the frozen waters of Disco Bay, Peary and Henson went ashore to make camp. Henson used his carpentry skills to build a large two-room house that served as expedition headquarters. The two men then set out to cross northern Greenland, in search of a shortcut to the North Pole. Henson enjoyed arctic life because, as an African American, he felt a new sense of equality with his fellow explorers that he never felt at home. His gift of language also allowed him to communicate easily with the Eskimos.

The trip was a great success—the exact latitude where the thick Greenland ice cap thinned out to sea water had been pinpointed. The two men had proven that Greenland was not a peninsula belonging to another land mass, but a great island unto itself. Peary also gained enormous practical knowledge on the expedition, such as adopting the fur costume of the Eskimos and building igloos instead of hauling heavy icy tents.

In 1899 a terrible misfortune struck Peary. Fearing another explorer might beat him to the pole, he raced across the ice in semi-darkness, freezing his feet.[7] When he took refuge in a barn, Henson helped to peel off Peary's sealskin boots. Two or three toes from each of Peary's feet clung to the hide, having snapped off at the first joints. Peary said, "A few toes aren't much to give to achieve the Pole."[8] The accident kept Peary bedridden for over a month. Then in the spring of 1899, he was able to walk with crutches. In 1901 Peary heard that his mother and infant daughter had died back home. In a moment of despair he said, "Now a maimed old man, unsuccessful after this most arduous work—has the game been worth the candle?"[9] In 1902 a surgeon operated on Peary's deformed feet, making cushions for his toe stumps so that Peary was able to walk with a gliding motion.

After a failed attempt to reach the pole—just one hundred miles short of the goal—time became

Robert Peary, on the deck of the *Barkentine Kite,* during one of the attempts at reaching the North Pole.

crucial. Peary, at fifty, and Henson, at forty, were getting too old for such arduous treks. If they did not soon achieve their goal, they probably never would. So in July 1908 Henson, Peary, and their party boarded the U.S.S. *Roosevelt* to begin their final assault on the North Pole. The trip was Peary's eighth into the wilderness.

In August they reached Etah, where they took on Eskimo helpers, coal, and supplies. Henson hunted for musk-ox, deer, and arctic hare and prepared the equipment for the relay march to the pole. Another team member, Donald MacMillan, said of Henson, "With years of experience equal to that of Peary himself [he] was indispensable to Peary."[10]

In February 1909 several large igloos—dubbed Crane City—served as base camp. Peary chose Henson to go with him on the final leg of the historic journey. "Henson must go all the way. I can't make it without him," Peary said.[11]

Henson, Peary, and four Eskimos—Ootah, Seegloo, Egingwah, and Ooqueah—were alone on the frozen Arctic Ocean, one hundred miles from the pole. For five days they raced toward their goal—against dangers of freezing or falling through thin ice and drowning. Finally Peary declared, "The pole at last! The prize of three centuries, my dream and my ambition!"[12] The date was April 6, 1909.

After the Peary party left the North Pole and re-turned to the United States, the men found a controversy raised by explorer Frederick Cook.

Cook claimed that he had reached the pole first in 1908. This controversy continues even today, but Peary and Henson are generally credited as the true discoverers of the North Pole.

For his achievement, Peary was made a Rear Admiral and honored around the world. He died on February 20, 1920, and was buried at Arlington Cemetery.

Henson wrote a book titled *A Negro Explorer at the North Pole*, and lived on a small pension in relative obscurity. Belatedly, in 1937, he was made an honorary member of the Explorers Club, and he received a Gold Medal from the Chicago Geographical Society. Henson died on March 9, 1955, and was buried in Woodlawn Cemetery in the Bronx, New York. At Henson's funeral Reverend Adam Clayton Powell, Jr., said that the "achievements of Henson are as important as those performed by Marco Polo and Ferdinand Magellan."[13]

In 1986 a United States postal stamp was issued honoring both Peary and Henson. In October 1987 President Ronald Reagan approved a request to move Henson's mortal remains next to Peary's in Arlington Cemetery. Henson's monument reads: "Matthew Alexander Henson, co-discoverer of the North Pole."

A twenty-one-gun salute hailed the moment when the two brave men who planted the American flag at the North Pole were once again together— this time at Arlington.

Richard Byrd

Richard Byrd

The Lonely Adventure

In 1900 twelve-year-old Richard Byrd had been invited by a family friend to visit the Philippines. His mother put him on a train from Washington, D.C., to San Francisco, California, where he would board the ocean liner *Sumner* for the voyage. During the trip a typhoon in the China Sea sent fifty-foot waves tearing the railings from the ship's deck. Once in the Philippines, Richard saw volcanoes erupting and criminals hanging from scaffolds. After celebrating his thirteenth birthday on the island, Richard headed home around Malaya, through the Indian Ocean, the Gulf of Aden, the Red Sea, and the Mediterranean Sea—finally docking in Boston, Massachusetts. This experience was unusual for a boy so young, but Richard was not destined to lead an ordinary life.

Richard Evelyn Byrd, Jr., was born in Winchester, Virginia, on October 25, 1888. He was an undersized boy nicknamed "Dickie." He responded to teasing by fighting for his rights. He actually tried to toughen himself by shunning warm clothing—even in winter.[1] At age fifteen, Byrd attended Shenandoah Military Academy. Then he spent two years at Virginia Military Institute and a year at the University of Virginia before entering the United States Naval Academy in 1908. The twenty-year-old midshipman excelled at mathematics and navigation. He also participated in tennis, football, track, and wrestling.

A broken ankle almost postponed Byrd's graduation in 1912, but in spite of the injury he struggled on to graduate with his class. However, he was left with a game leg that continued to trouble him. In 1915, at the age of twenty-seven, he married Marie Ames of Boston. In the Navy, Byrd received a medal for saving a drowning sailor, but he was still passed over for an adventurous assignment. Instead, because of his injured leg, Byrd was given a desk job. Byrd then asked for retirement. Only twenty-eight and without marketable skills, Byrd could not live on his disability pension. So he turned to a future where a bad leg did not matter as much—aviation.

Byrd was able to secure an appointment as a Naval Aviation cadet. He weighed only 135 pounds when he reported to the Pensacola Naval Air Station in Florida. The crash rate there was high—two or three a day.

Byrd first flew in a seaplane with double wings and a single engine. There was such terrible noise in the cockpit that Byrd had to stuff cotton in his ears. When the trainer gave Byrd the stick, the first-time pilot headed the plane right for the water. The craft dropped one thousand feet in a few seconds before the training pilot recovered control and safely landed the plane. Byrd was not discouraged, however. He was convinced that he could become a skilled pilot.

After six hours of flying on dual controls, Lieutenant Byrd soloed. As he attempted to land the seaplane, the craft struck the water, flipping over and bounding across the bay. Byrd kept on trying until he got it right. After much more training in his fragile wood-and-cloth plane, Byrd received his pilot's wings on April 7, 1917.

Twenty-nine-year-old Byrd began to dream of "firsts," such as being the first pilot to cross the Atlantic Ocean in a plane. He studied weather patterns and navigation charts for a possible transatlantic flight. In 1918 he requested permission to fly an NC-1 Navy plane on the trip, but his request was refused. The Navy was concentrating on helping fight World War I.

In 1925, after the war, Byrd commanded the Navy's flying unit that accompanied Donald MacMillan's arctic expedition, during which northern Greenland and Ellesmere Island were explored. In May 1926 Byrd set out on his first history-making adventure—the first flight over the North Pole. Byrd and fifty men boarded the *Chantier* in New York harbor and traveled five thousand miles to Kings Bay, Spitzbergen (now Svalbard Islands), north of Norway in the Arctic Circle. Byrd and his machinist's mate, Floyd Bennett, boarded one of the planes they had brought along. The plane, *Josephine Ford,* was loaded with food and supplies in case they were forced down. Lieutenant Commander Byrd set a straight course for the North Pole, using a sun compass as guide.

Byrd relieved Bennett as pilot during the flight of fifteen hours and fifty-one minutes. The pilots flew the plane at speeds of one hundred miles per hour. Though the starboard engine leaked fuel and the two men fought to stay awake, they circled the pole and then turned back, traveling 1,545 miles.

About his trip Byrd wrote, "America's claim to the North Pole was made certain tonight when, after a flight of fifteen hours and fifty-one minutes, Floyd Bennett, my pilot, and I returned safely from a flight to the North Pole."[2] The flight created international acclaim, making Byrd a hero. He was given the permanent rank of commander in the Navy.

Now Byrd turned to other challenges. He still wanted to be first to cross the Atlantic Ocean, and he wanted to fly to the South Pole. But while checking out another plane, the *America,* Byrd and Bennett were injured. By the time Byrd healed and before he could finish repairing his plane, Lindbergh made the historic first solo flight across the Atlantic. Byrd did cross the Atlantic in nine hours in *America*—winning more national and world acclaim—but he was not the first as he had hoped to be.

In 1928 Byrd planned his trip to the South Pole. However, when Floyd Bennett died of pneumonia, Byrd was deprived of his most-valued companion in adventure. But Byrd went ahead with his plans, using a fifteen-thousand-pound plane named the *Floyd Bennett.*

As a jumping off point to the South Pole, Byrd traveled to the Bay of Whales in the Ross Sea on the eastern side of New Zealand. On American Thanksgiving Day in 1928, Byrd headed for the South Pole—his goal at hand.

Antarctica is a core of high mountainous land. When Byrd's men leaped ashore they chased playful penguins. Then, on the edge of the Ross Ice Shelf, Byrd set out with his dogs and a portable radio. On January 1, 1929, Byrd located his base camp on a gentle slope, naming it "Little America." From there he surveyed twelve hundred square miles of unknown territory. Byrd and his men constructed buildings and radio towers. In March they explored with Byrd's sled dogs and his pet fox terrier, Igloo. The temperature was −38°F. On November 28 and 29 Byrd and three other men flew toward the South Pole—a hazardous flight against fierce wind currents.

"It is a confusing place, this imaginary point, the South Pole," Byrd wrote. "All time meridians converge here."[3] At the South Pole, Byrd opened his trap door and dropped an American flag, weighted with a stone from Floyd Bennett's grave.

Byrd returned to Little America and its harsh living conditions. A few motion pictures, card games, books, and a phonograph were all they had to break the monotony. But Byrd said, "There were times when Little America seemed about one of the happiest spots some of us had ever known."[4]

While reveling in his adventures, Byrd regretted the precious time he was losing with his son, Dickie, and his three daughters. Touched when his son gave him a favorite toy as a going-away gift, Byrd wrote, "What a wonderful thing to have come close to the mind of a child."[5] He wondered why he had chosen a life of far-off adventure, asking himself, "Why are you doing this? Can it be that the joy you get out of exploring is the decisive factor in all your plans, overpowering all other influences?"[6]

Byrd was a rear admiral when he returned to Little America for his most harrowing adventure. He had decided to man alone Bolling Advance Weather Base, located on a line between Little America and the South Pole. "It was one man's desire to know that kind of experience to the full, to be by himself for a while and to taste peace and quiet and solitude

On a later mission to the South Pole, Richard Byrd checks his
position with a sun compass while aboard an aircraft.

long enough to find out how good they really are,"[7] Byrd wrote.

Byrd's shack at Bolling was erected quickly in temperatures of −50°F. "We watched each other's faces for the dead white patches of frostbite," he said.[8] The other men then left Byrd alone in the winter of 1934. His world could be spanned "in four strides going one way and in three strides going the other," Byrd noted. "It was not a bright world."[9]

Byrd had a bed, one small table, a radio transmitter, food, tools, books, and clothing. A coal-burning caboose stove converted to burn oil would ward off the cold. During his solitude Byrd wondered about the meaning of life. He concluded that there was ". . . inexhaustible evidence for an all pervading intelligence. The human race, my intuition tells me, is not outside the cosmic process and it is not an accident."[10]

A treacherous threat then arose that almost took Byrd's life. He began suffering fits of depression. Soon his eyes hurt and his head ached. He grew thin and weak, and when he tried to drink water, milk, and sugar, he vomited. Byrd suspected that his illness was caused by fumes from a faulty stove. Falling to his hands and knees in the thick smoke, he crawled to the stove, turned it off, and collapsed on his bunk.

The next day when he awoke, Byrd's head and body ached. He relit the fire against the bitter cold and it burned yellow and red from faulty combustion. The stove had to be used sparingly lest it poison Byrd. Byrd refused to radio Little America for help, fearing those who would come to rescue him would be lost in the severe weather. He clung to the faith that he would somehow survive. He lived on dried lima beans, rice, turnip tops, corn, canned tomatoes, and cold cereal slaked with powdered milk. He went from 185 pounds to 125 pounds.

Byrd lived for the day when weather permitted the tractor team from Little America to reach him. At last, on August 11, 1934,—after five long months alone in his icy hut—Byrd spotted the searchlight of his rescuers.

As Byrd looked back at the weather station where he'd almost died, he said, "I did take away something that I had not fully possessed before. Appreciation of the sheer beauty and miracle of being alive and a humble set of values."[11]

Byrd headed a third Antarctica expedition from 1939 to 1941. During World War II, Byrd served in the South Pacific. In 1946 he led the largest Antarctica expedition in history—the United States Navy's Operation High Jump. Over four thousand men and a large force of ships and planes were involved. Byrd made his fifth and final trip in 1955, when the United States launched Operation Deep Freeze.

Byrd was a courageous explorer, but he was born a little late for his breed of person. After 1935 he never again could indulge in the hands-on type of adventure he enjoyed. He had made an outstanding contribution to arctic exploration, flying over both poles. He died on March 11, 1957, at the age of sixty-eight.

Charles Lindbergh

Charles Lindbergh

Spirit of St. Louis

The twenty-five-year-old pilot buckled his seat belt, pulled goggles over his eyes, and signaled the men at the wheels to remove the ropes. He revved on the throttle, and the tail of the small plane bobbed up. The wheels left the ground, then came down again, splashing through muddy water. Suddenly the plane was airborne, this time for good. Five thousand pounds of fuel, silver metal, and pilot had begun the incredible solo transatlantic journey of Charles Augustus Lindbergh, Jr.

Lindbergh was born in Detroit, Michigan, on February 4, 1902, but he was raised in Little Falls, Minnesota. The son of Congressman Charles Lindbergh, Sr., and schoolteacher Evangeline Land

Lindbergh, Charles Lindbergh enjoyed a boyhood filled with adventure and wilderness experiences.

As a boy, Lindbergh taught himself marksmanship. He roamed the woodland near his home, shooting partridges and studying woodcraft. He tamed a chipmunk and built a raft to pole himself down the Mississippi. He also learned to drive a Model-T Ford at age twelve and spent the summer of 1913 driving his father on campaign rounds.

Young Lindbergh had no interest in politics, but he heard his father bitterly denounce American involvement in World War I. Lindbergh, Sr., said, "War is paid for by the people. And what are we to gain? An enormous debt and the loss of valuable lives."[1]

At age thirteen, Lindbergh accompanied his father on an expedition to study the Mississippi River flooding. On a clinker-built boat (made with overlapping planks like a house), father and son were sunburned and bitten by mosquitoes. But young Lindbergh was made an honorary member of the Chippewa tribe, and the expedition was an adventure that he never forgot.

Lindbergh attended Little Falls High School. He did poorly in all his subjects except physics and mechanical drawing. In 1918 he left school to volunteer for farm work to help the World War I effort, receiving credit at school. Lindbergh earned his high school diploma in 1920, then spent a year at the University of Wisconsin.

Lindbergh enjoyed performing daredevil stunts

on his beloved motor bike, coasting down steep hills and then sailing through the air. Soon he began to think of *really* flying. When he saw an ad—placed by Nebraska Aircraft Co.—that offered flying lessons, he left college and headed for Nebraska.

After just eight hours in a Fokker Biplane (a plane with two sets of wings, one above the other), Lindbergh was hooked on flying. Nicknamed "Slim" for his tall lanky frame, Lindbergh went to work as a barnstormer (stunt pilot). In June 1922 Lindbergh made his first parachute jump. At this moment he conquered his fear of heights, describing the experience as one ". . . where life meets death on equal plane; where man is more than man and existence both supreme and valueless at the same instant."[2]

Billed on posters as "Daredevil Lindbergh," the young stunt pilot walked on the wings of planes during loops, his feet held in by straps. In 1923 he bought a used Curtiss Jenny (a wartime training plane with 90 horsepower and a top speed of 70 mph) for $500. The broken-down aircraft took Lindbergh all over the United States, as he lived the life of a footloose wanderer. To earn a living he charged passengers $5 for a ride in the plane.

In 1926, at the age of twenty-four, Lindbergh flew for a flying circus, earning $400 a month. Roman candles and streamers were attached to his airplane wings, and he gave nightly fireworks displays. Then he became an airmail pilot between

St. Louis and Chicago, and began dreaming of long-distance record-breaking flights.

Lindbergh heard of the Orteig Prize being offered to any flier or group of fliers who crossed the Atlantic Ocean—from New York to Paris or Paris to New York—without a stop. He was sure he could do it, and the $25,000 prize sounded good too! But Lindbergh needed financial backing to get the kind of plane he needed. The money came from a group of St. Louis businesspeople who wanted to promote St. Louis by participating in such a history-making flight.

Lindbergh accepted the offer of the small Ryan Aircraft Company in San Diego, California, to build his special plane for $10,580 within sixty days. Ryan was so small that every employee—from president to the latrine cleaner—took part in building the plane. On April 26, 1927, the plane, christened *Spirit of St. Louis,* was rolled from its hangar. The craft was strange-looking, with wheels hanging below its body and flat untapered wings. The pilot's view was blocked by a huge gasoline tank, so to see Lindbergh would have to lean out and look sideways. But this was the plane in which he thought he could fly to Paris.

On May 20, 1927, at 7:54 A.M., the small silver monoplane began its flight from Roosevelt Field in New York. A New York tabloid reported: "Flyin' fool hops today!"—as the young pilot carried only a compass, sextant, five sandwiches, a gallon of water, and a chart balanced on his knees. He even omitted a radio to save weight!

Lindbergh was glad he was flying alone, recalling an old proverb his father had often repeated. "One boy's a boy. Two boys are half a boy. Three boys are no boy at all."[3] Lindbergh had only himself to rely on and be concerned about as he skimmed close to the sea. When he flew over Newfoundland, he realized that the next land he would see would be two thousand miles away in Ireland.

In the fourteenth hour of the flight, Lindbergh saw icebergs—lustrous white pyramids rising from the sea. He flew higher to avoid them, and bone-chilling cold seeped in around him. Shiny ice began dangerously to coat the wings of the plane. Lindbergh carefully descended, weaving in and out of the clouds. A quick plunge to de-ice the wings could have sent him into a fatal tailspin. Lindbergh said, "There are periods when it seems I'm flying through all space, through all eternity."[4]

In the eighteenth hour of the flight, Lindbergh was at the midway point. He was getting weary, and to stay alert he had to vigorously shake his head, flex his muscles, and bounce and stamp his feet. He leaned out the window and gulped in cold air to try to stay awake. A little later he felt pins and needles in his arms and legs, and he was glad for the rain that pelted him when he stuck his head from the cockpit. He was now flying half-blind, half-asleep, and half-awake—drifting in and out of a fantasy world.

In the thirty-first hour of flight, Lindbergh spotted land. He dove down to see Irish villagers waving and he thought, "Here are human beings! Here's a human welcome! I've never seen such beauty before. Fields so green. People so human!"[5]

Lindbergh passed over Cornwall and later, as the sun dipped over the horizon, the *Spirit of St. Louis* soared over the French coast. Lindbergh had broken the world's distance record for a nonstop airplane flight. At last, when he was almost at his destination, he ate the first food since leaving New York. He grabbed a sandwich, devoured it quickly, and started to toss the brown wrapper from the plane. But he stopped himself, crumpled the wrapper, and put it in his bag. "I don't want the litter from a sandwich to symbolize my first contact with France!" he said.[6]

At 9:52 P.M. Lindbergh sighted the Eiffel Tower and circled it. Then, in the darkness, he located Le Bourget airport and touched down on floodlighted concrete. He had flown from New York to Paris in thirty-three and one-half hours, landing on May 21, 1927. Neither Lindbergh's life nor aviation would ever be the same again.

Lindbergh emerged from the plane as dozens of outstretched hands reached for him. They grabbed his arms, legs, and body. His plane trembled from the press of humanity, and he heard fabric ripping as souvenir hunters quickly went to work. Lindbergh was hoisted atop the crowd. He was "in the center of

Charles Lindbergh poses next to his plane, the *Spirit of St. Louis.* It was on this plane that he made his history-making flight.

an ocean of heads that extended as far into the darkness as I could see," he said.[7]

From around the world gifts and salutations, including two million pieces of fan mail, descended on Lindbergh. Towns, streets, mountains, and even newborn babies were named for him. When he returned to America he was welcomed by a parade down New York's Fifth Avenue, with three to four million people cheering.

President Calvin Coolidge gave Lindbergh the Distinguished Flying Cross, and Congress voted him the Medal of Honor—the first time the medal was ever awarded for a peacetime feat. The young hero reacted to all the praise by saying, "I was so filled up with this hero guff. I was ready to shout murder."[8] This dislike of publicity and resentment of the press continued throughout Lindbergh's life.

In the spring of 1929 Lindbergh married twenty-one-year-old Anne Morrow, Ambassador Dwight Morrow's daughter. Lindbergh had met her during a goodwill flight to Mexico. By mid-1929 Anne Lindbergh was a qualified navigator and radio operator. In 1930 tragedy struck the Lindberghs when their nineteen-month-old son, Charles Lindbergh, III, was kidnapped and killed.

Heartbroken by the loss of their son and bitter against the media,[9] the Lindberghs sailed for Europe in 1935. During their four years there, Lindbergh traveled to Germany and expressed admiration for the German military. He was awarded the Service

Cross of the German Eagle, a high Nazi civilian decoration. Lindbergh returned to the United States in 1939. He opposed the United States entering World War II. His isolationist pro-German speeches and expressions of anti-Semitism angered many Americans, including President Franklin Roosevelt.

When Pearl Harbor, Hawaii, was attacked, Lindbergh tried to enlist in the military, but Roosevelt blocked him—deeming him unfit to wear the uniform of his country. Lindbergh found a civilian job helping American pilots master new planes. Friends then sneaked him into the South Pacific, where he was soon engaging in dogfights against the Japanese. Lindbergh took part in fifty combat missions.

After World War II, President Dwight Eisenhower promoted Lindbergh to Brigadier General in the Air Force. Lindbergh's book, *Spirit of St. Louis,* won a Pulitzer Prize. He still believed entering World War II was a mistake, writing in 1970: "In order to defeat Germany and Japan, we supported the still greater menaces of Russia and China, which now confront us in a nuclear weapon era."[10]

Lindbergh spent his final years promoting conservation. He died on August 9, 1974. He was survived by his wife and four sons. Although Lindbergh's political views were controversial, there can be no doubt of the young pilot's awesome courage. Lindbergh almost single-handedly launched the intercontinental aviation age with his 1927 flight into history.

Amelia Earhart

Amelia Earhart
For the Fun of It

In the summer of 1908 eleven-year-old Amelia Earhart went to the Iowa State Fair with her father. They walked to the south end of the fairground, and her father hoisted her to his shoulders for a better view of the strange contraption on display. There were two broad boards held together with thin pieces of wood and a bulky gasoline motor. A man wearing goggles climbed aboard, and sputtering, crackling sounds filled the air. The contraption—called a plane—began to move. It rose in the air to the gasps and cheers of onlookers. The blue-eyed child, perched on her father's shoulders, watched the plane as it circled overhead. Much later, Amelia would give her whole heart to aviation.

Amelia Earhart was born July 24, 1897, in

Atchison, Kansas. She was always adventuresome, choosing a faster boy's sled over a slower girl's sled. She enjoyed lying on her stomach and going "belly whomping." She also would invariably jump a fence rather than go through the gate. Her favorite toy was a wooden donkey rather than a doll.[1] She loved the game of "map-traveling" with her sister. The girls would randomly place their finger on a spot on the map and then imagine getting there.

Amelia's favorite school subjects were reading, science, and geography. During her early teens, Amelia lived in a private railroad car with her parents since her father, a railroad claims adjuster, traveled for his job. Amelia attended six high schools, finally graduating from Chicago's Hyde Park High School in 1916. The caption under her yearbook picture read: "The girl in brown who walks alone."[2] It was an apt comment on the personality of a young woman who would be comfortable being alone during most of her life.

Amelia next attended the Ogontz School near Philadelphia. The headmistress there described Amelia as "always pushing into unknown seas in her reading."[3]

On a 1918 trip to Toronto, Canada, World War I came home to Amelia Earhart. She saw the war wounded—"men without arms and legs, men who were paralyzed and men who were blind."[4] Earhart decided to leave Ogontz School before graduation so that she could work as a nurse's aide at Spadina Military Hospital in Toronto. During ten-hour shifts she cared for the wounded, scrubbed floors, and did whatever else was needed.

One day Earhart attended the Toronto Exposition, and—watching a stunt pilot spin, roll in the air, and do loops—she decided to learn to fly.[5] But the dream was expensive, costing $1,000 for ten hours of flight instruction. Earhart could not yet afford the lessons, so she returned to college. In 1920 she earned her bachelor's degree at Columbia University in New York City. Afterward she traveled to Los Angeles, California.

Earhart attended another air show, at Dougherty Field, in Los Angeles. At age twenty-two, she took her first ride in a plane. Dressed in dark goggles and helmet, she flew up to two thousand feet. She was now more determined than ever to become a pilot.

Earhart took a job at the phone company to pay for flying lessons from Neta Snook ("Snooky"), the first woman to graduate from the Curtiss School of Aviation. Snooky told Earhart to trim her long hair so that her helmet would fit better. From that day forward Earhart kept her hair short. The eager student learned the parts of the plane and the instrument panel, and then—with Snooky at the dual controls—Earhart began to fly.

Earhart wanted to learn flying stunts before she soloed. So she practiced looping, diving, flying upside down, and performing barrel rolls. Then it was time for her solo. Earhart bought a black, shiny, patent leather jacket for her solo flight. However, when the big day came, she was fearful—not of flying, but of landing!

Earhart climbed into her plane, flew to five thousand feet, dove, turned, looped in figure eights, and then dropped down for a landing. She had conquered her fears. At twenty-three, Earhart became one of the few women in the world licensed to fly at that time. Now she wanted her own plane. "Pilots are always dreaming dreams," she said of herself.[6]

Earhart bought a small plane for $2,000 and participated in air shows. She yearned to earn her living flying, but nobody would hire a woman pilot. So she went to work at Denison House, a settlement house for immigrants in New York City, teaching Syrian and Chinese children. Settlement houses were places where immigrant families met to socialize and learn English, among other things. While there, she received a phone call offering her the chance to be part of a crew flying across the Atlantic Ocean. A wealthy woman, Mrs. Frederick Guest, wanted a woman pilot aboard the transatlantic flight—even though a man, Wilmer Stutz, would be the pilot.

Earhart got the job, not only because of her flying skills, but also because she bore a striking resemblance to Charles Lindbergh—so much so that she was nicknamed "Lady Lindy." On a sunny June morning in 1928, Earhart, Stutz, and a mechanic left New York for Europe aboard a plane named *Friendship.* Since she was not the pilot, Earhart was stunned by the publicity descending on her when the plane landed. Although she wrote a book about the experience, *Forty Hours, Twenty Minutes*, she felt unworthy of all the attention.

Earhart was determined to do some real flying as a pilot. She made a cross-country flight over the United States, becoming the first woman to have flown across a continent and back again. In 1930 Earhart broke the altitude record for autogiros (helicopter-like crafts), flying as high as 18,415 feet. Job offers for the attractive, blue-eyed, tousled-haired pilot poured in. Earhart became a symbol of a new womanhood.

In 1931 Earhart married wealthy publisher George Palmer Putnam, who had helped select her for the *Friendship* flight. In May 1932 she became the first woman to fly across the Atlantic Ocean alone, five years after Lindbergh's historic flight. The trip was wild and sometimes frightening, as the plane bucked like a wild horse. Icy wings once sent the plane into a near-fatal dive. However, Earhart regained control just in time—only one hundred feet above the water! Congratulations poured in from around the world, and Earhart was invited to the White House.

Earhart wrote another book in 1932, *For the Fun of It*, and she taught at Purdue University. She opposed rigid sex roles, saying, "I have known girls who should be tinkering with mechanical things instead of making dresses, and boys who would do better at cooking than engineering."[7]

In 1935 Earhart became the first person to fly

from Hawaii to California. She wrote: "It was a night of stars. Stars hung outside my cockpit window near enough to touch."[8] In the same year she became the first person to solo anywhere over the Pacific Ocean, and the first pilot to solo both the Atlantic and Pacific Oceans. Then she became the first person to solo from Los Angeles to Mexico.

Earhart now felt ready to fulfill her most ambitious dream—to fly around the world. She bought a two-motor, red-winged Lockheed, named *Electra*. Then she hired Irishman Fred Noonan as her navigator (he had flown the Pacific Ocean seventeen times), and pinned a shamrock on her shirt for good luck.

Earhart knew the flight would be dangerous. "Someday," she would say, "I'll get bumped off. There's so much to do, so much fun here, I don't want to go but. . . ."[9] Another time she said, "When I go, I'd like best to go in my plane, quickly."[10] The possibility of death during one of her flights was never far from her mind.

Earhart's route for her around-the-world flight was Miami, Florida, to Puerto Rico to South America; then across the Atlantic to Africa, east to Pakistan, east to Australia, and east to New Guinea. Next she would fly eastward over the most perilous leg of the journey—the uncharted south central Pacific Ocean—to Howland Island, a tiny refueling stop. Finally she would fly to Honolulu, Hawaii, and back home to Oakland, California, where her husband would be waiting.

In June 1937 Earhart and Noonan climbed into

Amelia Earhart had an ambitious dream: to fly around the world.

Electra and left Miami for San Juan, Puerto Rico, the first officially recorded leg of the trip. Earhart and Noonan then flew along the eastern coast of South America. They took off from Natal, Brazil, and flew across the Atlantic Ocean, landing on the west coast of Africa. Then they flew across Africa to Massawa, Ethiopia. From there they flew across the Red Sea to land in Karachi, Pakistan. Next they flew to Calcutta, India; Rangoon, Burma (now Myanmar); then to Singapore; Darwin, Australia; and finally, Lae, New Guinea. Earhart telephoned her husband. When asked if she was having a good time, she said, "You betja! It's a grand trip!"[11]

Earhart had traveled over five continents, crossed the equator four times, and flown twenty-two thousand miles in forty days! She was tired and ready to go home, but there was one more hurdle to cross—reaching Howland Island. After that she would be home free.

At 10:00 A.M. on July 2, 1937, Earhart and Noonan took off for the 2,556-mile flight to Howland Island, a sandy knoll about one mile long and half a mile wide. No one had ever made this flight before. Howland Island was a dot surrounded by seven thousand miles of ocean—the smallest navigational error could cause the pilot to miss it entirely!

At Howland Island, gasoline tanks waited to refuel the *Electra* for the next leg to Honolulu. Earhart was estimated to reach Howland Island eighteen hours after leaving New Guinea. The United States

Coast Guard cutter *Itasca* waited off the island to give Earhart radio bearing.

At 2:45 A.M. on July 3, Earhart radioed "cloudy and overcast." Later her voice came back, loud and clear, but high and frantic. "We must be on you. But cannot see you. Gas is running low. Been unable to reach you by radio. We are flying at altitude one thousand feet." Still later Earhart said, "We are circling but cannot hear you."[12] At this point she had been in the air for twenty hours—two hours past the time she should have landed at Howland Island. The last voice contact was broken and frenzied, and then there was silence.

The *Itasca*, together with a battleship, four destroyers, a minesweeper, and an aircraft carrier searched for sixteen days, but they found no trace of Amelia Earhart, Fred Noonan, or *Electra*. When she vanished, Earhart was about three weeks from her thirty-ninth birthday.

Earhart left a letter to be opened in case she failed on her round-the-world flight. She wrote:

> Please know I am quite aware of the hazards. I want to do it because I want to do it. Women must try to do things as men have tried. When they fail their failure must be but a challenge to others.[13]

In the many decades since the disappearance of Amelia Earhart, numerous theories have been advanced about her fate. Probably the exact truth of how she died will never be known, but there will never be doubt about her courage.

Jacqueline Cochran

Jacqueline Cochran
Beyond the Speed of Sound

Jackie had been in school only three days when a teacher wielding a ruler sent her flying from the classroom—not to return for a year. In that time she hunted, fished, and crabbed in the marshes of northern Florida. "I just ran wild—a real harum-scarum ragamuffin,"[1] Jackie said. When she finally returned to school, a different kind of teacher awaited her—Miss Bostwick.

> She gave me a little dress to wear which she had ordered by mail. Now I could hold my head up with the other children from the right side of the tracks. The priest taught me godliness and Miss Bostwick taught me the next thing to godliness which is cleanliness. She lifted the horizons for me and gave me ambition.[2]

Jacqueline Cochran was not sure where or when she was born—perhaps between 1905 and 1908. Her birth parents—whom she never knew—gave her to another family, who kept her but never adopted her. Her new parents had two boys, Joe and Henry, and two girls, Myrtle and Mamie. Jackie slept on a blanket or quilt on the floor and ate mullet (fish) and beans, with an occasional bit of sowbelly (fat salt pork). Blackeyed peas were a rare treat, and butter and sugar were never seen. Sometimes all Jackie had to eat was what she could find in the forest. Hunger was constant. Once, from a nearby farm, she ate boiled sweet potatoes that were being prepared to feed the pigs.

Jackie and the family she lived with traveled by train across southern Florida—through mill towns such as Bagdad, Millville, and Panama City—in search of work for the father and oldest son. Jackie remembered African-American children coming on the train to sell chicken and bread. The food smelled wonderful, but her family had no money to buy it. At the next stop they walked three miles, through sand bogs up to their ankles, to the sawmill camp that offered work. Jackie did not own a pair of shoes until she was about eight.

As she grew older, Jackie earned extra money helping mothers care for their children. One Christmas she entered a raffle to win a beautiful big doll with curly blonde hair, big brown eyes, and pearly skin. She won the doll, but when she took her treasure home, her foster mother made her give the doll to an older sister's new baby. Jackie made up her mind to someday right that wrong.

When she was about eight, Jackie got a job at a cotton mill in Columbus, Georgia, for six cents an hour. At that time she bought her first pair of shoes. Before she had turned ten, Jackie was promoted to inspection room supervisor over fifteen other children. When another child asked Jackie what she wanted to do when she grew up, Jackie piped up, "I'm going to be rich. I'll wear fine clothes, own my own automobile, and have adventures all over the world."[3]

At about age eleven, Jackie left the cotton mill to work as a cook and cleaning woman for a well-to-do beauty shop owner. There she learned to mix shampoos and wave hair. At about age fourteen, Jackie lived alone at a boarding house in Montgomery, Alabama, giving permanent waves at a nearby salon. She bought an old Model-T and learned to repair it herself.

Although she had only a second-grade education, Jackie Cochran entered a Catholic nursing school and studied for two years. She lacked the education to pass the State Board of Nursing Examination, so she worked as a doctor's assistant. Helping the doctor in the amputation, by saw, of a patient's mangled leg changed Cochran's career plans. She returned to the beauty shop business.

Cochran felt no strong ties to the family she had lived with as a child, but she always helped them financially. When she was about eighteen, she decided to find a name for herself. She picked up a phone book and "ran my finger down a list of names and decided on Cochran. It had the right ring to it. It sounded like me."[4] Jacqueline Cochran was now her name by choice.

Cochran moved to Biloxi, Mississippi, and operated a beauty shop at the Edgewater Beach Hotel. In 1929 she headed for New York, rented a room at Broadway and 79th Street, and began working at a salon. Soon after she had settled in New York, the foster sister whose baby had gotten Cochran's prize doll years before, came to visit, asking for help. Cochran helped her, but asked for the return of—and received—the beloved doll. She was never to part with the doll again.

Cochran became friends with a business tycoon named Floyd Odlum. Although he was fourteen years older than she was, they fell in love. Odlum urged Cochran to learn to fly, so she took three weeks of instruction at Roosevelt Field in New York in the summer of 1932. "At that moment when I paid for my first lesson, a beauty operator ceased to exist and an aviator was born," she said.[5]

Flying instructor "Husky" Lewellyn gave Cochran a few instructions and then let her attempt to land; she was successful. On the third day Cochran went up for her first solo flight, though she did not yet know much about planes. Lewellyn called her a "born flyer, one of the smartest gals in the air I ever saw."[6]

Cochran read about Ryan Flying School in San

Diego, California. Soon, traveling alone, she drove her Chevrolet west to enroll. In six months she experienced ten years' worth of trial-and-error flying, landing on beaches and in open areas all over southern California. A special tutor gave her the math knowledge she lacked, and she passed her exam for a commercial pilot's license.

In 1935 Cochran started Jacqueline Cochran Cosmetics—her own line of beauty products, including moisturizers, makeup, and hair dyes. Then in 1936 in a quiet ceremony in Kingman, Arizona, Jacqueline Cochran and Floyd Odlum were married. They bought a ranch in Indio, California.

On New Year's Day in 1937 Cochran's close friend, Amelia Earhart, was at the ranch discussing her upcoming round-the-world flight. Cochran expressed grave fears about the risks involved, but Earhart said she simply had to go ahead.[7] When news came that Earhart was lost at sea in the summer of 1937, Cochran went to a cathedral in Los Angeles, California, to "say a prayer for my friend, and to light candles for her soul which had gone from this earth."[8]

Since 1934 Cochran had been entering air races, and in 1938 she entered the Bendix Transcontinental Air Race. Flying from Los Angeles to Cleveland, Ohio, Cochran rose to twenty-five thousand feet trying to get above the weather and the ice that coated her cockpit windshield. As she dropped down in altitude, the engine stopped. So Cochran leaned over to switch to another gas tank. Suddenly the plane veered over on one wing, almost flying on its side! Cochran went into a dangerous spiral, straightening just in time to avoid crashing. She flew on to win the Bendix race.

By this time World War II was looming, so Cochran organized a group of American women pilots to go to Great Britain. While in London, she lived alone in a little house behind Harrod's department store. She became the first woman to pilot a bomber across the Atlantic. By this time Cochran had already set a national altitude record for women. She was unafraid as bombs rained over the London skies.

Once, as a dogfight raged overhead, Cochran wrapped herself in a blanket before windowpanes shattered around her. A nearby house exploded, but she said, "I used to think that my time would come up when my number was up, so I went about my business openly."[9]

The women Cochran trained transported planes from factories and picked up downed aircraft, freeing men for combat roles. While America was at war, Cochran trained one thousand women pilots at Fort Worth, Texas, for the same tasks. She started the Women's Air Force Service Pilots (WASPs)—the first female military pilots in United States history. Cochran's pilots flew sixty million miles during the war, and for her work, Cochran received the Distinguished Service Medal in 1945.

At the end of World War II, Cochran traveled

Jacqueline Cochran stands by her plane before a flight in 1939.

around the world, visiting Japan as a lieutenant colonel in the USAF reserve. In 1948—while in Dallas, Texas, on a business trip—she piloted a seriously ill, then senatorial candidate, Lyndon B. Johnson to the Mayo Clinic in Rochester, Minnesota. Forever after President Johnson referred to Cochran as "the pretty gal that saved my life."[10]

Cochran was now in her forties and eager for new adventures. She had been in the center of aviation, but now it seemed as though the jet phase was passing her by. Cochran used her influence to work with jet test pilot General Chuck Yeager in the Canadian-built F-86—the fastest plane in the world at that time. She spent many hours at Edwards Air Force Base, California, in jet trainers with Yeager. "She was a Sherman Tank at full steam," Yeager said of Cochran. "She was as nuts about flying as I was."[11]

In 1953 Cochran was proficient enough to fly at Mach 1—the speed of sound. She climbed to forty-five thousand feet, then started a full-power, almost vertical dive for the airport. "I was hanging face down diving at Mach 1 with my blood surging into my brain. I pulled out of that first dive through the sound barrier, exhilarated, exhausted."[12]

Cochran saw the sky grow dark blue and the sun appear as a bright globe, while stars could be seen at noon. But she could not hear the sound of her own plane since she was outrunning sound. Cochran said that she was impressed with the immensity of space. Being so close to space and those noonday stars convinced her that there must be a divine order of things.[13]

In 1953 President Dwight Eisenhower presented Cochran with the Harmon Trophy for Outstanding Female Pilot of the Year. In 1961 Cochran set eight major speed records. Then in May 1964 she flew a Lockheed F-104 jet Starfighter to break the women's international speed record at 1,429.297 miles per hour. Throughout the 1960s Cochran continued to set speed records.

In 1970 Cochran tried to fly a Lockheed helicopter, but the onset of heart trouble frustrated her plans. She began having seizures and blackouts. In 1971 doctors implanted a pacemaker and told her that she must stop flying. In response, she immediately bought a motor home in which to travel. In 1976 her husband Floyd Odlum died in Cochran's arms. It had been a long and happy marriage. Four years later, in August 1980, Jacqueline Cochran died.

Cochran was buried with her rosary and the doll she won as a child. By coincidence jets streaked overhead. An old friend, Father Charles M. Depiere, said, "I'd like to presume that there was some divine pilot guiding her heavenward."[14]

Cochran's achievements are impressive. She held more speed, distance, and altitude records than any other pilot of either gender in aviation history! She also rose from the grimmest of poverty to become an aviation legend.

Neil Armstrong

Neil Armstrong
One Giant Leap

The lunar module (LM), dubbed *Eagle*, left the command module (CM) *Columbia*, and began its descent to the Moon. "How does it look?" NASA (National Aeronautics and Space Administration) in Houston, Texas, radioed. "The *Eagle* has wings," Neil Armstrong answered.[1] The automatic landing system was taking the *Eagle* into a crater that was the size of a football field and contained a large number of boulders and rocks. Armstrong gripped the hand controller. He now had to fly as he had never flown before. He had to hand-fly the rest of the way to the surface of the Moon.[2]

The *Eagle* was dropping twenty feet per second. Armstrong slowed it to nine feet per second. Then he saw that, beyond a field of boulders and slightly to the left, the rocks were thinning out. There was a smooth flat area in which he could land. The *Eagle* had just ninety seconds of fuel left. The lunar module swayed gently as the thrusters (rocket engines) obeyed Armstrong's commands. The landing was smooth, and Neil Armstrong's voice sounded calm, confident, and clear. "Houston, Tranquility Base here. The *Eagle* has landed."[3] The time was 4:17 P.M. Eastern Daylight Time on July 20, 1969.

Neil Alden Armstrong was born on August 5, 1930, on his grandparents' farm near Wapakoneta, Ohio. Seven thousand people lived in the area of rich farmland and rolling hills. "My father tells me about going out to the Cleveland Airport when I was two years old to see the 1932 air races," Armstrong recalled. "So I must have been a staunch aviation fan before I was even conscious of it."[4]

Armstrong's father also took Neil for his first plane ride at the age of six. They flew in a Ford tri-motor (a single-winged, three-motored plane), nicknamed the "Old Tin Goose." At age nine, Neil built model planes powered by rubber bands. The Great Depression of the 1930s left little money around the Armstrong home. So in building his models, Neil had to use straw, paper, and whatever wood scraps he could find. Still, Neil's planes seemed to fly faster and farther than the models that other children were making. To test his model planes, Neil used a fan to build a wind tunnel in his basement.

Neil was an exceptional student. By the time he completed first grade, he had read about ninety books. He then skipped second grade after testing at a fifth-grade reading level. A neighbor owned the most powerful telescope in town, and Neil spent many hours looking at the red planet of Mars and the rings of Saturn. Neil also collected issues of *Air Trails* magazines, and he kept a notebook of everything he read about flying. The Wright Brothers had grown up near Neil's hometown, and he was aware of their flying exploits.

In his early teens, Neil worked at the local market, pharmacy, and hardware stores. "I don't think I ever got paid more than forty cents an hour on any of these jobs," Armstrong recalled.[5] As a high school freshman, Neil worked at Neumeister's Bakery. Being small for his age, which was a factor in his getting this job in the first place, Neil was able to crawl inside the bakery's mixing vats at night to clean them. He was then responsible for turning out one hundred and ten dozen doughnuts every night.

The shy, blue-eyed teenager decided to take flying lessons, which cost $9 an hour. Eventually he saved enough money from all his various jobs to pay for the lessons. He soloed and received his student pilot's license on his sixteenth birthday, August 5, 1946—before he had his driver's license.

Neil Armstrong joined the United States Navy in 1947, and attended classes at Purdue University in West Lafayette, Indiana. He had completed just two years when the Navy ordered him to Pensacola, Florida, for flight training as a Naval Air Cadet. In 1950, Armstrong became the youngest man in his unit to fly combat missions in Korea; Armstrong piloted a Navy panther jet.

"The work was air-to-ground bridge breaking, train stopping, tank shooting," Armstrong recalled. [6] Once he narrowly escaped death when the wing of his jet clipped a cable stretched across a North Korean valley. After coaxing his crippled jet back to friendly territory, Armstrong successfully ejected from his now out-of-control plane. A Jeep driver rescued him, taking him to a nearby United States Marine base. Before the end of the Korean War, Armstrong had flown seventy-eight combat missions and was awarded three Air Medals.

In 1952 Armstrong returned to Purdue University to finish his bachelor's degree in flight engineering. There, he met Janet Shearon, and they were married in 1956.

After college, in 1955, Armstrong worked as a research pilot at Lewis Flight Propulsion Lab in Cleveland, Ohio. From 1956 to 1962 Armstrong worked at Edwards Air Force Base, California, as a test pilot. Neil and Janet bought an old cabin without electricity overlooking the San Gabriel Mountains. Soon two sons and a daughter were born. (The daughter, named Karen, died of a brain tumor before the age of three.)

At Edwards, Armstrong flew faster than the

speed of sound in the X-1 and the X-15. These jets were half-rockets and half-planes, designed to fly into the outer limits of Earth's atmosphere. At the time it was the closest that humans had come to space travel. Armstrong flew the X-15 at speeds of four thousand miles per hour, forty miles above the earth. From that altitude, Earth looked round. Between 1952 and 1962 Armstrong was an engineer and experimenter, and he made major contributions to the development of new methods of flight.

When NASA was looking for astronauts, Neil Armstrong applied. In 1962 he was accepted and stationed in Houston, Texas.

On March 16, 1966, Armstrong commanded the *Gemini 8* mission. Also on board was astronaut David Scott. The flight, which ran ten hours and forty-two minutes, marked the first successful docking with a target vehicle. For the first time Armstrong saw Earth from outer space. And he was awed by the vivid blue oceans and snowy clouds as well as the blackness of space.

Disaster almost ended the *Gemini 8* mission when the two crafts began pitching wildly and then spinning. Armstrong detached the *Gemini* capsule from the target vehicle, but soon the capsule was spinning faster than one revolution per minute. Radio contact with Earth was lost. It was nail-biting time at NASA until Armstrong's cool voice said that the craft had been steadied. Armstrong's piloting skills in this situation made a strong impression on people at NASA. Without this mission and the subsequent pioneering flights of *Gemini 9, 10,* and *11,* there would have been no *Apollo* landing on the Moon.[7]

Armstrong returned to test flying for two more years. Then, on January 9, 1969, when three men were chosen for the most ambitious space journey yet—a landing on the Moon—it was announced that the flight commander would be Neil Armstrong. Rounding out the *Apollo 11* crew were Michael Collins, the command module pilot, and Edwin "Buzz" Aldrin, Jr., lunar module pilot.

By the end of May 1969 Armstrong and the other astronauts had trained long hours in the simulators (gigantic machines located on the Earth that imitated conditions in space). Armstrong had the extra chore of flying the lunar landing training vehicle (LLTV).

On July 16, 1969, Armstrong, Aldrin, and Collins donned their bulky spacesuits and headed to the launchpad. Liftoff went perfectly, and *Apollo 11* was underway. Reaching the Moon would take four days. Once there, Armstrong and Aldrin would fly the *Eagle* to the moon's surface. First the command module (CM) *Columbia* would make twelve revolutions around the Moon, landing the lunar module (LM) *Eagle* on the thirteenth.

Armstrong took over the computer and landed the *Eagle* himself. He swung his left foot to the surface of the moon at 7:56 A.M. Pacific Daylight Time.

Neil Armstrong on the morning of the historic *Apollo 11* spaceflight, July 16, 1969.

He then uttered his now famous words: "That's one small step for a man . . . one giant leap for mankind."[8]

Armstrong said the surface of the Moon "appears fine grained, almost like a powder. I can kick it loosely with my foot."[9] He began gathering samples of lunar soil—a "quick grab" of sample material, about two pounds, retrieved with a butterfly net. Armstrong took this quick sample so that if a sooner than planned launch from the Moon was necessary, they would at least have a small sample.[10]

President Richard Nixon spoke to Armstrong and the other men by radiotelephone:

> Because of what you have done the heavens have become part of man's world and, as you talk to us from the Sea of Tranquility, it inspires us to redouble our efforts to bring peace and tranquility to the earth.[11]

For more than two hours Armstrong and Aldrin moved in slow bounding strides on the Moon's surface. They planted the American flag, took photographs, and collected rock samples. Then the two men blasted off from the Moon and docked with *Columbia*, which had been orbiting the Moon waiting for them. Returning to Earth four days later, *Columbia* arched gracefully over Australia and the Coral Sea, coming down in the Pacific Ocean. In about an hour Armstrong and his crew were taken aboard a helicopter and flown to the U.S.S. *Hornet* aircraft carrier.

Armstrong, Aldrin, and Collins were honored in a New York parade the size of which had not been seen since Charles Lindbergh's welcome from his transatlantic solo flight. The three men were awarded the Presidential Medal of Freedom—the highest United States civilian award—from President Nixon. Later they visited twenty-two countries and were greeted by thousands of people.

Neil Armstrong and his fellow crew members had been the first people to see the sight of Earth rising above the Moon's horizon. The dream first voiced by President John F. Kennedy to land men safely on the Moon by 1970 had been achieved. But, in spite of all the acclaim that Armstrong received, he remained a quiet rather shy man who did not enjoy public adulation.

In 1970 Armstrong resigned from NASA to resume a private life, which included teaching aeronautical engineering. In the years since his historic landing on the Moon, Armstrong has worked in research and development. He also enjoys soaring in a glider through the clear midwestern skies.

Neil Armstrong and his crew left on the moonscape a bronze plaque that reads:

> Here Men from the planet Earth first set foot upon the Moon, July, 1969 A.D. We came in peace for all mankind.

Sally Ride

Sally Ride

Blast Off

A born athlete, Sally Ride spent much of her free time playing baseball and football with neighborhood boys. She was often the only girl chosen for their rough-and-tumble sandlot games. Sally fantasized about someday becoming a great baseball player with the Los Angeles Dodgers. She also played tennis, and read spy and science fiction novels. In addition, she followed the space program, recalling later, "I could tell you exactly where I was when John Glenn went into space, and when Neil Armstrong walked on the moon."[1]

Sally Kristen Ride was born in Encino, California, on May 26, 1951. She was the eldest of two daughters born to Dale and Joyce Ride. In 1960, when Sally was nine, the Rides spent a year in Europe. Sally's parents, both teachers, tutored the girls, and when Sally returned to school she was well ahead of her class.

Sally began winning weekend tennis tournaments and was eventually the eighteenth ranked junior player in the United States. At Portola Junior High School, Sally studied science and math. In 1964 she attended Westlake High School in Beverly Hills, California, on a scholarship. Sally was inspired by Dr. Elizabeth Mommaerts, a science teacher. As a high school student, Sally studied chemistry, physics, trigonometry, and calculus. She entered Swarthmore College in Swarthmore, Pennsylvania, for a year, then transferred to Stanford University in Palo Alto, California. She continued to play tennis, but she gave up any dreams of having a tennis career. Her mother said, "Sally simply couldn't make the ball go just where she wanted it to go. And Sally wouldn't settle for anything short of excellence in herself."[2]

At Stanford, Ride studied physics and English literature, especially enjoying Shakespeare. "I really had fun reading Shakespeare's plays," Ride said. "It's kind of like doing puzzles. You had to figure out what he was trying to say."[3] In 1973 she graduated with two degrees, a B.A. in English and a B.S. in physics. She then entered Stanford's masters program, specializing in astrophysics. Ride studied the physical and chemical characteristics of celestial matter, focusing on rays given off by stars.

In 1977 when Ride completed work for her

doctorate in astrophysics, she looked in the classifieds of the Stanford University paper. She imagined a research or teaching position for herself. But she noticed that NASA (National Aeronautics and Space Administration) was looking for young scientists to become mission specialists who would conduct experiments aboard the space shuttle. Women were being encouraged to apply. Successful applicants would have to be under forty years old, normal height and weight, good eyesight, and team players with poise, self-confidence, and analytical minds. Ride seemed to fit the requirements well.

Another applicant for a place on the 1978 astronaut team was tall, red-haired Steve Hawley, an astronomer. He later became Ride's husband.

When Ride reported to Lyndon Johnson Space Center in Houston, Texas, for a detailed personal interview, she met with doctors and NASA officials. She passed the stress tests well. On the morning of January 16, 1978, Ride received a phone call from NASA. "Well, we've got a job for you if you are still interested in taking it."

Ride responded with an enthusiastic "Yes, Sir!"[4] Ride received her doctorate from Stanford and reported to the astronaut team as Dr. Sally Ride. She would train with thirty-four other new astronauts. She wore a T-shirt with the letters TFNG on it— "Thirty-five new guys."[5]

Ride had done research on free-electron lasers, which was one of the reasons she was chosen. NASA officials hoped her work could be used to develop a method of sending energy from a space station back to Earth.

Much of Ride's training involved getting used to the rigorous demands of space and learning survival skills. She had to scuba dive in cold water and practice the "drop and drag" exercise. Wearing her spacesuit and strapped into an open parachute, Ride was dropped by a moving boat. She had to free herself from the parachute harness, while being dragged on her stomach and back, and then swim free. This would prepare her for survival if the astronauts had to land in the water after re-entry into Earth's orbit.

Ride also spent long hours preparing for the feelings of weightlessness. She snorkeled in a "neutral buoyancy chamber," a tank filled with water. In addition she rode in the KC-135 aircraft, nicknamed the "vomit comet" by other astronauts because it caused nausea. The plane climbed to a high altitude, then dove down. For thirty seconds there was zero gravity. Most astronauts got sick, but Ride did not.

In April 1982 Ride was given her mission in the seventh space shuttle flight—*Challenger* STS-7. Ride would be the first American woman in space. George W. S. Abbey, director of flight operations at NASA, said of her, "Sally Ride is smart in a very special way. You get people who can sit in the lab and think like Einstein, but they can't do anything with

Sally Ride talks to ground controllers from the flight deck of the
Space Shuttle *Challenger.*

it. Sally can get everything she knows together and bring it to bear where you need it."[6]

Ride's job in the flight would be to operate a fifty-foot-long robotic arm (RMS) that she had helped develop. Ride practiced until the arm "got to be as natural as using tweezers on a noodle."[7]

On July 24, 1982, Sally Ride and Steve Hawley were married. Ride flew her own plane to the wedding in Kansas. Hawley took two space shuttle flights in 1984 and 1986. In 1987 Ride and Hawley were divorced.

June 18, 1983, was the day that Dr. Sally Ride and her fellow crew members stepped out onto the pad beside the thirty-story-high space shuttle. *Challenger*, commanded by Robert Crippen, blasted off with the largest human payload to date—four men and one woman. The shuttle carried two communications satellites that would be returned to earth after tests, and two satellites to be placed in orbit. The shuttle also took into space twenty experiments designed by high school and university students.

On the first day of the six-day flight Ride launched ANIK-C, a Canadian communications satellite to route television, Telex, and telephone signals throughout North America. The next day the Indonesian satellite, Palapa B., was launched to provide telephone service to one million people in southeast Asia.

On the fifth day in space Ride and Colonel John M. Fabian used the robotic arm. Ride pressed buttons to manipulate the spindly arm and clawlike hand as it grabbed the satellite, pulled it from the cargo bay, and released it into space. Over the next nine hours Ride and the crew experimented with the robotic arm. It operated perfectly, and the *Challenger* mission was called 96 percent successful.

On June 24, the sixth and last day in space, the crew prepared for re-entry. On a clear day the shuttle re-entered Earth's atmosphere and glided down in the desert. Ride and her fellow astronauts had made ninety-seven orbits around Earth and traveled over two million miles. President Ronald Reagan spoke to the crew, saying to Ride, "You were the best person for the job."[8]

Ride and the shuttle crew received the keys to New York City. Sally herself became an instant celebrity upon her return to Earth. She lectured and appeared on television, often speaking to young people. In 1984 Ride ran in the Olympic torch relay. Even though Ride thought that too much was being made of the fact that she was the first American woman in space, she good naturedly answered endless questions about herself.

Ride made her second space journey on October 15, 1984. The thirteenth shuttle mission on *Challenger* was again commanded by Robert Crippen. The main task was to launch an Earth Radiation Budget Satellite, using the robotic arm. The mission was successful, and Ride joined the rest of the crew in a press conference from space.

On January 28, 1986, tragedy struck the space

shuttle program. The *Challenger* exploded about seventy-three seconds after takeoff, killing the entire crew of seven. President Reagan appointed a twelve-member commission to investigate the *Challenger* explosion, including Dr. Sally Ride.

Ride and her fellow commissioners learned that the fatal explosion was caused by the failure of rubber seals known as O-rings. Ride helped prepare the 256-page report that criticized safety procedures, engineering faults, and human errors.

In 1986 Ride published her book *To Space and Back*, dedicating it to the crew lost in the *Challenger* explosion. Ride was also inducted into the National Women's Hall of Fame that year. She also wrote the Ride Report, in which she suggested four possible directions for the future of the space program. The Earth's environment itself could be explored by space satellites or the solar system could be explored. She wrote that permanent or semi-permanent outposts to the Moon could be built or humans could eventually land on Mars.

In May 1987 Ride, then thirty-six, left the astronaut corps to return to private life as a scientist. She is currently director of the California Space Institute in La Jolla, California. She is also a professor of physics at the University of California at San Diego. Ride declines most interviews. Public demands upon her time continue, but she explains:

> If I were going to continue to be a public figure and be part of public projects and do a

lot of speaking, I couldn't in good conscience take a job at a university. Most of what I am doing is related to science and scientific research.[9]

Ride works in an unmarked office. She focuses on plasma physics and free-electron lasers.

A NASA administrator, James Fletcher, summed up her contribution to space with: "The nation owes her a debt of gratitude. Her flight as the first American woman in space firmly established an equal role for women in the space exploration program."[10]

Ride's own comments about what she did in space reveal much about her spirit and the spirit of all adventurers. "The thing that I'll remember most about the flight," she said, "is that it was fun. In fact, I'm sure that it was the most fun that I will ever have in my life."[11]

Those who know Dr. Sally Ride may doubt her prediction, but none question the joyful enthusiasm that she developed as she soared into space.

Guion Bluford, Jr.

Guion Bluford, Jr.

Beyond the Barriers

The guidance counselor from Overbrook High School visited the Bluford family to tell them that their son Guion was not college material. He might do better as a mechanic or carpenter, the Blufords were told. True, schoolwork did not come easy to young Guion (guy-on). He had to work hard at it.[1] But Guion had always built detailed model planes, and when he played table tennis he studied the way the ball rolled with the keen eye of a physicist. He was determined to go to college, and nothing that a guidance counselor said would stop him.

Guion Stewart Bluford, Jr., was born November 22, 1942, in Philadelphia, Pennsylvania. He was the eldest of three boys. The Blufords, an African-American family, lived in a middle class, racially mixed neighborhood. Guion's father, Guion Bluford, Sr., was a mechanical engineer. His mother, Lolita Bluford, taught special education. Both parents urged their sons to do their best.

As a boy, Guion worked crossword puzzles, had a paper route, and reached the rank of Eagle Scout in the Boy Scouts. He also collected photographs of planes as a hobby.

Bluford's high school physics teacher said of him, "He would sit very quietly until I began asking really hard and challenging questions. Then he would come alive."[2]

Aerospace was in its infancy during Bluford's teens, and he was very interested in space satellites such as the Russian Sputnik. He liked math and science courses, was captain of the chess team, and a member of the science club. He graduated from Overbrook High School in 1960, and entered the aerospace engineering program at Pennsylvania State University, State College, Pennsylvania.

Although this was a decade when the civil rights movement was very influential, Bluford did not participate in marches or protests. He spent all his time studying calculus, engineering, and other college courses. One of his engineering professors, Barnes McCormick, said of Bluford, he was a "very religious person, easygoing, careful in what he said."[3]

After submitting his senior thesis on the flight of a boomerang, Bluford graduated in 1964 from Penn State with a B.A. in aerospace engineering. Bluford had been active in ROTC (Reserve Officers' Training Corps) and graduated as a distinguished Air Force ROTC graduate. He decided he wanted to be a pilot, so he joined the Air Force. Bluford went to boot camp at Otis Air Force Base in Cape Cod, Massachusetts. His first ride in an Air Force T-33 convinced him that he wanted to become an Air Force pilot.

Bluford married fellow Penn State graduate Linda Tull, and their first son—named Guion Stewart, III—was born in June 1964. James Trevor, the second son, was born in October 1965.

Bluford took pilot training at Williams Air Force Base in Arizona, earning his wings in 1965. At that time the Vietnam War was raging, and good pilots were in demand. Bluford joined the F-4C fighter squadron based in Cam Ranh Bay in South Vietnam. The twenty-three-year-old pilot served with the 557th Tactical Fighter Squadron. He flew the phantom jet on 144 combat missions, including 65 over North Vietnam. Bluford logged three thousand hours of flying time and became a military hero. He won ten Air Force medals, the Vietnam Cross of Gallantry with Palm (a palm added to a military decoration indicates the wearer has for a second time merited the basic decoration), and Vietnam Campaign and Service medals.[4]

Back in the United States, Bluford was considered one of the best pilots in the country. He was sent to Sheppard Air Force Base in Texas to teach cross-country and acrobatic flying. He used seven different jets in his work, logging over five thousand hours in the air.

Bluford received a Master of Science degree from the Air Force Institute of Technology in 1974, and a doctorate in aerospace engineering with a minor in laser physics in 1978. Working at Wright-Patterson Air Force Base in Ohio, he felt that he had achieved a childhood goal—he was an aerospace engineer.

In 1978 Guion Bluford took the next step to advance as far into space as humans were going—he applied to be an astronaut. NASA (National Aeronautics and Space Administration) seemed the perfect place to combine his flying and engineering skills. Bluford was one of over eighty-eight hundred applicants for thirty-five spots. A few weeks after he applied Bluford was accepted. For the next six months he underwent the rigorous NASA physical training as well as studying the shuttle system.

Asked about the prospect of being the first African-American in space, Bluford said:

> It might be a bad thing if you stop and think about it. It might be better to be second or third because then you can enjoy it and disappear—return to the society you came out of without someone always poking you in the side.[5]

Bluford would be working closely on moving payloads in and out of the space shuttle cargo bay, so he spent three months working on the mechanical arm. At the end of the year he was a full-fledged astronaut. He began flying in the shuttle simulators to get used to a feeling of space. Simulators are Earth-bound machines that mimic space flight conditions.

Bluford said of his work, "It gives me a chance to use all my skills and do something that is pretty exciting. The job is so fantastic, you don't need a hobby. The hobby is going to work."[6] However, Bluford also found time for jogging, raquetball, handball, and tennis as well as reading and photography.

Bluford was assigned as mission specialist on STS-8, *Challenger's* third flight into space. The first African American to enter space received much publicity. Like all trailblazers, Bluford received media and popular attention. But none of it was sought by the quiet scientist and pilot.

On August 30, 1983, at 2:32 A.M. Eastern Daylight Time, the orbiter *Challenger* lifted off in darkness—the first "night" launch for a space shuttle. The crowd gathering to watch included two hundred and fifty of the nation's top African-American educators and other Americans. For the thousands who watched the sight was marvelous. Orange flames and billowing white vapor lit the sky as far away as Miami, about two hundred miles to the south.[7]

For Bluford and the rest of the five-person crew, the tasks of living in space began. Bluford enjoyed fruit cocktails, roast beef sandwiches, and anything that stuck to the plate—such as macaroni and cheese. Food such as peas were a problem because they quickly flew away.

On the second day in space Bluford deployed the INSAT-1B, an Indian communications satellite. It was designed to help predict monsoons and floods as well as to improve India's telephone and television systems. "The deployment was on time, and the satellite looks good," Bluford reported.[8]

During the flight Bluford ran on a treadmill while wired to monitors. NASA was trying to learn ways of reducing the effects of Space Adaptation Syndrome Sickness (nausea and dizziness during space travel). Bluford and fellow astronaut Dale Gardner also conducted experiments with human and animal cells to help develop medicine to fight diabetes, dwarfism, and heart disease.

After the ninety-sixth orbit the *Challenger* headed back toward Edwards Air Force Base in California's Mojave desert for the first night landing of a shuttle. The mission was declared a success. Seeing the hundreds of well wishers, Bluford said:

> I'm really humbled tonight to see so many people out here to welcome us back. I feel very proud to be a member of this team and I think we have a tremendous future with the space shuttle—I mean *all* of us.[9]

Bluford's second trip into space was on October 30, 1985. Again he blasted off aboard *Challenger*'s mission STS-61-A, the German Space Lab—carrying eight crew members, including three Europeans.

Guion Bluford was a mission specialist aboard the Space Shuttle *Challenger.* Here, he uses a treadmill designed for spaceflight as part of a medical test.

This was the largest crew aboard a shuttle to date. It was also the first shuttle under the command of a foreign power—Germany. Germany had paid NASA $65 million to use the shuttle to launch its Message Relay satellite. Seventy-six other experiments were also aboard. After 111 orbits around Earth in 169 hours, the *Challenger* came roaring down at Edwards Air Force Base.

In 1986 the *Challenger*, on which Bluford had previously ridden twice, exploded, causing delays in the space program. During his time off, Bluford received a master's degree in business administration from the University of Houston at Clear Lake to prepare himself in business matters.

When the space program resumed on April 28, 1991, Bluford was aboard the new orbiter *Discovery*. The crew of mission STS-39 gathered aurora (lights seen in night skies near geomagnetic poles) as well as celestial and environmental data. They also launched and recovered experiments in space. After 134 orbits in 199 hours, Bluford and his fellow crew members completed another great success.

Bluford's final space flight was launched December 2, 1992, aboard *Discovery* STS-53—a secret mission. The five-person crew deployed military satellites under the Military Man-in-Space program (which uses space for military purposes such as surveillance of military sites in other countries). After landing at Edwards Air Force Base, Bluford had logged a total of 688 hours in space.

The six-foot-tall, one hundred and eighty pound space veteran's early NASA portrait featured a smiling man with jet black hair. Now the portrait featured a smiling proud pilot with hair speckled gray. Bluford's dark brown eyes continued to shine with the joy of adventure.

In July 1993 Bluford left NASA and accepted a position as vice president and general manager of the engineering service division of NYMA.INC. in Greenbelt, Maryland.

As President Ronald Reagan predicted when he warmly welcomed Bluford back from space, other young African Americans were now astronauts. Bluford had said, "I'm sure we will hire more in the future."[10] And by the summer of 1992, five African Americans had joined NASA.

A soft-spoken man who never sought the fanfare that followed his ascent as the first African American in space, Guion Bluford, Jr., told six hundred high school students in Harlem, New York:

> What I want to pass on to you is that it's very important to set high goals for yourself and realize that if you work hard you will get them. I want you to be the future astronauts.[11]

Christa McAuliffe

Christa McAuliffe
Touching the Future

Little Christa Corrigan loved to roam around. One day she climbed on her tricycle, and without telling anybody, simply set out for town. She was nearly three years old and her dog Teddy bounded at her side. Suddenly Christa was in the middle of a busy street, with traffic coming from all directions. Teddy ran in frantic circles, barking in alarm. Then the dog took a firm hold of Christa's clothing and pulled her back to the safety of the sidewalk. Her parents practiced extra vigilance after that incident because it seemed as though their little girl was absolutely fearless in her quest for new experiences.

Sharon Christa Corrigan was born September 2, 1948, in Boston, Massachusetts. When Christa was six months old a severe intestinal ailment almost took her life. She was saved by a new medicine, but the medical bills impoverished the young family. The McAuliffes lost their home, and had to move into an apartment and start over again.

As a child, Christa helped tend her four younger siblings. As a young girl, her favorite television program was *Superman,* and she was very interested in space. Christa admired people such as President John F. Kennedy and Alan Shepard, who made America's first manned spaceflight in 1961. Christa saved newspaper stories about spaceflights, and her toy satellites often ended up on neighbors' roofs. She attended Marian High, a Catholic co-educational school, where she met Steven James McAuliffe, her future husband.

One of Christa's teachers, Sister Mary Denisita, said of her, "Her face was very alive; very interested. You could tell by looking at her that she was excited about everything life held before her."[1]

As a teenager, Christa was active in charity work, including food drives for the poor. She said that if she was not helping, "I felt like I was cheating myself and everyone else I had a chance to help."[2]

When Christa and Steve were just sixteen they decided to be married after they both finished college. Christa attended Framingham State College, majoring in American history and secondary education. An honor student, she recalled, "I developed a healthy distrust for authority. I guess I started hoping I could change the world."[3] Steve attended Virginia Military Institute in Lexington, Virginia.

On August 23, 1970, after they had both graduated from college, Christa and Steve McAuliffe were married at St. Jeremiah's Church. Both were twenty-one and both were unemployed. Between them they had $500, so their honeymoon was a highway trip in an old orange Volkswagen.

McAuliffe soon found a job as a full-time substitute teacher at Benjamin Foulois Junior High, where she taught history to eighth graders in Morningside, Maryland. Steve attended Georgetown University Law School nearby. The McAuliffes lived in a small apartment with a leaky roof and plenty of cockroaches. Their furniture came from flea markets and their sofa was inflatable. Still, Christa McAuliffe said, "We thought we had everything we needed."[4]

Before long McAuliffe was teaching at Thomas Johnson Junior High. An enthusiastic teacher, she played the guitar and led her students in singing folk songs of the day. McAuliffe took her students on field trips to historic sites and to actual trials in court, where her husband—now a lawyer—was trying cases.

In September 1976 son Scott Corrigan was born. The family moved to an aging Victorian house in Concord, New Hampshire. Soon after daughter Caroline was born. As a young Girl Scout, McAuliffe had spent happy summers in New Hampshire. So moving north was a pleasant experience.

McAuliffe taught at Concord High School and introduced a class called "The American Woman." She drew attention to many women who made important contributions, but were virtually unknown. She told her students, "Any dream can come true if you have the courage to work at it."[5] She also told her classes, "I ask only two things of you. Be yourself and do the best you can."[6]

In August 1984 NASA (National Aeronautics and Space Administration) began its search for the first citizen passenger in space. President Ronald Reagan, as his way of paying tribute to America's teachers, decided the citizen would be a teacher. Any teacher in good health, with good vision, and five years of classroom experience could apply. Edward Campion, NASA's public affairs officer said, "We're looking for the person who can do the best job of describing their experience on the shuttle to the most people on earth."[7]

Christa McAuliffe got one of the twenty-five page applications, which required one hundred and fifty hours to complete. In answer to the question "Why do you want to be the first U.S. citizen in space?" McAuliffe said in part:

> I cannot join the space program and restart my life as an astronaut, but this opportunity to connect my abilities as an educator with my interests in history, and space is a unique opportunity to fulfill my early fantasies—I watched the space age being born and I would like to participate.[8]

In total, 11,500 teachers applied—including 79 from New Hampshire. Each state was given two finalists, and McAuliffe was one of the New Hampshire pair. If she were chosen, her space project would be a detailed journal of the experience. All the state finalists arrived in Washington, D.C., to compete over six days. By June 28, 1985, the list would be narrowed to ten. Three weeks later the first teacher in space would be chosen.

On June 27 McAuliffe learned that she was among the final ten. She was then sent to NASA facilities in Houston, Texas, to undergo rigorous physical tests and interviews. She passed both the claustrophobia (fear of being in small tight places) and weightlessness tests. She impressed the judges with her poise. "She was articulate and enthusiastic. The one we thought could talk to five thousand people at the National Education Association convention and impress them," one judge said.[9]

On July 19, 1985, Christa McAuliffe was announced as the choice for America's teacher in space. She received an Oscar-sized trophy of a student looking up to a teacher who was pointing to the stars. Back home in Concord, there was great celebration. McAuliffe returned to her family and was met by many well-wishers and a bagpipe band. The next day she rode in an open convertible as thousands cheered along Concord's main street.

In September 1985 McAuliffe began intensive training as an astronaut. She also began preparing the lessons that she would teach from space. Her lessons included walking the students through life on the space shuttle and instructing them on the history of flight. McAuliffe also planned to explain the benefits of space. Using props such as bottles of oil and water as well as candy and marshmallows, she would show that neither liquids nor solids separate in weightlessness. After the space flight, McAuliffe was scheduled to visit classrooms all over America.

In December 1985 McAuliffe spent the holidays with her family. The whole family attended church together on Christmas. In January 1986 she returned to Florida for the space flight.

McAuliffe's fellow crew members were a diverse group—Judith Resnik, an electrical engineer; Ronald McNair, a physicist; Ellison Onizuka, an engineer; Gregory Jarvis, an engineer; Michael Smith, the pilot, and Dick Scobee, commander. All of them waited out the weather delays in the launching of the *Challenger*. Unseasonable cold gripped Florida, with temperatures dipping to 24°F.

McAuliffe planned to teach from space on days four and five. "No teacher has ever been better prepared to teach a lesson," she said five days before the flight.[10]

Each member of the crew was allowed to carry up to twenty-four ounces of mementos. McAuliffe took her husband's class ring from the Virginia Military Institute, her daughter's cross and chain, and her son's stuffed frog Fleegle. She also carried a

The crew of the Space Shuttle *Challenger* included (from left to right) Ellison Onizuka, Michael Smith, Christa McAuliffe, Dick Scobee, Gregory Jarvis, Ronald McNair, and Judith Resnik.

T-shirt bearing her favorite motto: "I touch the future. I teach."

On January 28, 1986, McAuliffe was presented with a polished Delicious apple—a gift from the technical crew. "Save it for me," she said, "and I'll eat it when I get back."[11] As the space shuttle crew donned their helmets, it was so cold that McAuliffe clapped her arms. One crew member said, "My nose is freezing!"[12]

The families of the crew, including Steve McAuliffe and their two children, watched from the roof of Launch Control Center. Thousands more watched from the ground and millions viewed the scene on television—including McAuliffe's students in Concord. The main engines started, and the shuttle was launched at 11:38 A.M. Electrifying excitement turned to shock and disbelief when the shuttle exploded at forty-six thousand feet! The *Challenger* vanished in a cloud of billowing smoke and orange fire.

As news of America's worst space disaster spread, Christa McAuliffe's grief-stricken students gathered in a gymnasium at Concord High to mourn and pray. On January 30 thousands attended a memorial service at Framingham State College. A large wreath of white carnations was dropped from a helicopter into the ocean where debris from the space shuttle fell.

A private funeral mass was conducted for Christa McAuliffe by the priest who married her and Steve. Six months later, when the astronauts' remains were recovered, McAuliffe was laid to rest in Concord,

New Hampshire, in a grave overlooking a winding river in evergreen hills by two freshly planted maple trees.

Millions of dollars in scholarships were donated in McAuliffe's honor. The Christa McAuliffe Center was established at Framingham State College. From Hawaii to New York—and even to distant Pakistan—schools, libraries, airports, bridges, and even mountains were named for her.

The Rogers Commission investigating the space shuttle tragedy concluded that O-rings (rubber seals like washers) failed, partly due to the extreme cold. Gases as hot as 5,000°F leaked out, triggering the explosion. Redesigned rockets were recommended.[13]

Eight years after McAuliffe's death, her mother Grace Corrigan finished a book of memories, *A Journal for Christa.* Corrigan said that bells were installed in Christa's church, St. Jeremiah's, in her daughter's honor. "Listen," Corrigan said. "Those are Christa's bells. Can you hear them?"[14] Like the bright and shining life of Christa McAuliffe, the bells ring with faith and hope.

Chapter Notes

Preface

1. Robert T. Hohler, *"I Touch the Future": The Story of Christa McAuliffe* (New York: Random House, 1986), p. 14.

2. Jane Hurwitz and Sue Hurwitz, *Sally Ride: Shooting for the Stars* (New York: Fawcett Columbine, 1989), p. 99.

Chapter 1

1. Orville and Wilbur Wright, "The First Airplane to Fly Successfully," *America: Library of Original Sources*, Vol. X, Veterans of Foreign Wars in the U.S. Publishing Co., 1925, p. 185.

2. Tom Crouch, *The Bishops' Boys: A Life of Wilbur and Orville Wright* (New York: W. W. Norton & Co., 1989), p. 14.

3. Orville Wright, *How We Invented the Airplane* (New York: David McKay, 1953), p. 19.

4. Fred Howard, *Wilbur and Orville: A Biography* (New York: Alfred A. Knopf, 1987), p. 16.

5. Crouch, p. 118.

6. Orville and Wilbur Wright, p. 197.

7. Orville Wright, "How We Made the First Flight," *Flying*, Vol. 11, No. 11, December 1913, p. 10.

8. Wilbur and Orville Wright, *Miracle at Kitty Hawk: The Letters of Wilbur and Orville Wright*, ed. Fred C. Kelly (New York: Farrar, Straus, 1951), p. 118.

9. Harry Comb, *Kill Devil Hill* (New York: Houghton Mifflin Co., 1979), foreleaf.

10. H. Guyford Stever and James J. Haggerty, *Flight* (New York: Time-Life Books, 1965), p. 18.

11. Wilbur and Orville Wright, *The Papers of Wilbur and Orville Wright, Including Chanute-Wright Letters*, ed. Marvin W. McFarland (New York: McGraw-Hill, 1953), p. 953.

Chapter 2

1. Matthew Alexander Henson, *A Negro Explorer at the North Pole* (New York: Frederick A. Stokes, 1912), p. 132.

2. Robert E. Peary, *North Pole* (New York: Frederick A. Stokes, 1910), p. 287.

3. Dennis Rawlins, *Peary at the North Pole: Fact or Fiction* (New York: Robert B. Luce, Inc., 1973), p. 31.

4. Ibid., p. 35.

5. Robert E. Peary, *Northward Over the "Great Ice"* (New York: Frederick A. Stokes, 1898), p. 508.

6. Henson, p. 3.

7. Rawlins, p. 42.

8. Ibid., p. 43.

9. Ibid., p. 48.

10. S. Allen Counter, *North Pole Legacy* (Amherst, Mass.: The University of Massachusetts Press, 1991), p. 64.

11. Bradley Robinson, *Dark Companion* (New York: Robert M. McBride, 1947), p. viii.

12. John Edward Weems, *Peary, the Explorer and the Man: Based on His Personal Papers* (Boston: Houghton Mifflin Co., 1967), p. 270.

13. "Matt Henson Mourned by Thousands," *Amsterdam News* (New York), March 19, 1955, p. 1.

Chapter 3

1. Edwin P. Hoyt, *The Adventures of Admiral Byrd* (New York: The John Day Co., 1968), p. 5.

2. Lt. Commander Richard E. Byrd, "Byrd Flies Over the North Pole and Back to Base," *Los Angeles Times*, May 10, 1926, p. 1.

3. Richard Byrd, *Little America* (New York: G. P. Putnam's Sons, 1930), p. 341.

4. Ibid., p. 207.

5. Ibid., p. 6.

6. Ibid.

7. Admiral Richard Byrd, *Alone* (New York: G. P. Putnam's Sons, 1928), p. 4.

8. Ibid., p. 38.

9. Ibid., p. 53.

10. Ibid., p. 161.

11. Ibid., p. 295.

Chapter 4

1. Leonard Mosley, *Lindbergh: A Biography* (New York: Doubleday, 1976), p. 16.

2. Ibid., p. 39.

3. Charles Lindbergh, *The Spirit of St. Louis* (New York: Charles Scribner's Sons, 1953), p. 191.

4. Ibid., p. 364.

5. Ibid., p. 463.

6. Ibid., p. 485.

7. Ibid., p. 496.

8. Mosley, p. 122.

9. Ibid., p. 200.

10. Charles Lindbergh, *The Wartime Journals of Charles Lindbergh* (New York: Harcourt Brace Jovanovich, 1970), p. xv.

Chapter 5

1. Jean L. Backus, *Letters From Amelia: An Intimate Portrait of Amelia Earhart, 1901–1937* (Boston: Beacon Press, 1982), p. 14.
2. Ibid., p. 35.
3. Ibid., p. 25.
4. Ibid., p. 44.
5. Ibid., p. 14.
6. Amelia Earhart, *Last Flight* (New York: Harcourt Brace and Co. Inc., Orion Books edition, 1988), p. 1.
7. Backus, p. 184.
8. Earhart, p. 14.
9. Ibid., p. xvi.
10. Ibid., p. xvii.
11. Ibid., p. 105.
12. Peggy Mann, *Amelia Earhart: The First Lady of Flight* (New York: Coward McCann Inc., 1970), p. 120.
13. Earhart, p. 134.

Chapter 6

1. Jacqueline Cochran, *The Stars at Noon* (Boston: Atlantic Monthly Press, 1954), p. 11.
2. Ibid., p. 18.
3. Jacqueline Cochran, *Jackie Cochran: Autobiography*, with Mary Ann Bucknum Brinley (New York: Bantam Books, 1987), p. 35.
4. Ibid., p. 49.
5. Cochran, *The Stars at Noon*, p. 41.
6. Cochran, *Jackie Cochran*, p. 72.
7. Vincent V. Loomis, with Jeffrey L. Ethell, *Amelia Earhart: The Final Story* (New York: Random House, 1985), p. 48.
8. Cochran, *Jackie Cochran*, p. 142.
9. Ibid., p. 188.
10. Ibid., p. 254.
11. General Chuck Yeager and Leo Janos, *Yeager: An Autobiography* (New York: Bantam Books, 1985), p. 212.
12. Cochran, *Jackie Cochran*, p. 308.
13. Ibid., p. 348.
14. Ibid.

Chapter 7

1. *Time*, 60th Anniversary issue, October 5, 1983, p. 142.
2. Alan Shepard and Deke Slayton, *Moon Shot: The Inside Story of America's Race to the Moon*, introduction by Neil Armstrong (Atlanta: Turner Publishing Co., 1994), p. 23.
3. Ibid., p. 27.

4. Neil Armstrong, Michael Collins, and Edwin E. Aldrin, *First On the Moon: A Voyage with Neil Armstrong, Michael Collins, Edwin E. Aldrin,* written with Gene Farmer and Dora Jane Hamblin (Boston: Little, Brown and Co., 1970), p. 143.

5. Ibid.

6. Ibid., p. 145.

7. Dr. Wernher von Braun, *Space Frontier* (New York: Holt, Rinehart, & Winston, 1971), p. 68.

8. Armstrong, et al., p. 51.

9. Marvin Miles and Ruby Abramson, "Walk on Moon," *Los Angeles Times,* July 21, 1969, p. 1.

10. Ibid.

11. Ibid.

Chapter 8

1. Jane Hurwitz and Sue Hurwitz, *Sally Ride: Shooting for the Stars* (New York: Fawcett Columbine, 1989), p. 15.

2. Sally Ride with Susan Okie, *To Space and Back* (New York: Lothrop, Lee, and Shepard, 1986), p. 16.

3. Susan Okie, "Interview with Sally Ride," *Washington Post,* May 7, 1983, p. 1.

4. Hurwitz and Hurwitz, p. 18.

5. Ibid., p. 23.

6. NASA *Information Summary*—Space Shuttle Mission Summary—1981–1983, STS Missions 1—9, PMS 003-A (KSC), p. 6.

7. *Chicago Tribune,* Part XII, April 24, 1983, p. 1.

8. Hurwitz and Hurwitz, p. 45.

9. Ibid., p. 67.

10. Bruce V. Bigelow, "Astronaut Ride Takes Small Quiet Steps at UCSD," *San Diego Union Tribune,* March 16, 1994, p. E2.

11. "Sally Ride," *Current Biography,* October 1983, p. 320.

Chapter 9

1. *Washington Post,* August 21, 1983, p. 1.

2. Scott Minerbrook, "Guion Bluford, Jr.," *Newsday,* August 29, 1983, Part II, p. 4.

3. Ibid.

4. NASA *Biographical Data* (Houston: Lyndon B. Johnson Space Center, June 1993), p. 1.

5. *Current Biography,* Vol. 45, No. 9, p. 31.

6. Ibid.

7. *Biographical Data,* p. 1.

8. NASA *Information Summaries,* PMS, 003-A (KSC), January 1988, p. 6.

9. *Current Biography,* p. 5.

10. Deborah Johns Moir, "Reaching Beyond the Stars," *U.S. Black Engineer*, Summer 1992, p. 30.

11. *Current Biography*, p. 5.

Chapter 10

1. Robert T. Hohler, *"I Touch the Future": The Story of Christa McAuliffe* (New York: Random House, 1986), p. 29.

2. Ibid.

3. Ibid., p. 35.

4. Ibid.

5. Ibid., p. 52.

6. Ibid., p. 47.

7. Ibid., p. 60.

8. Ibid., p. 64.

9. Ibid., p. 125.

10. Malcolm McConnell, *Challenger: A Major Malfunction* (New York: Doubleday & Co., Inc., 1987), p. 87.

11. Ibid., p. 223.

12. Ibid., p. 224.

13. William J. Broad, "Back in Space," *1989 World Book Yearbook* (New York: World Book Inc., 1989), p. 45.

14. Joseph P. Kahn, "A Graceful Look Back at McAuliffe," *San Diego Union*, November 2, 1993, p. E-3

Index